Twenty Thousand Miles to See a Tree
An Around the World Bicycle Journey

Cindie Cohagan

Drifting Sands Press

Twenty Thousand Miles To See A Tree:
An Around the World Bicycle Journey

Cindie Cohagan

Published by:
Drifting Sands Press
4022 East Evans Dr.
Phoenix, Arizona 85032
www.driftingsandspress.com

All Rights Reserved. No part of this book shall be reproduced or transmitted in any form or by any means, electronic or mechanical, including photocopying, recording or by any information storage and retrieval system, without written permission from the author, except short quotations for review or academic reference, with copies thereof sent promptly to the publisher.

Copyright © 2014 by Cindie Cohagan
ISBN 978-0-9850096-8-7
Library of Congress Control Number: 2014941153
Photo Credit: All photography by Tim Travis or Cindie Cohagan
Cover photo taken near Quito, Ecuador
Back cover photo taken in the Adelaide Hills, Australia.

Disclaimer
This book describes the author's experience while traveling around the world by bicycle and reflects her opinions relating to those experiences. Some names haver been changed to protect the privacy of the people I mentioned.

Table of Contents

TABLE OF CONTENTS	3
PROLOGUE	7
ACKNOWLEDGEMENTS	9
Podcasts and Radio	9
Interviews and Presentations	9
Part 1 - Introduction	**12**
CHAPTER 1 BICYCLING THIRTY THOUSAND MILES THROUGH TWENTY-THREE COUNTRIES	13
The Trip	15
The Continents	16
North and Central America	16
Arizona	*16*
Mexico	*17*
Guatemala	*17*
Honduras	*17*
Nicaragua	*17*
Costa Rica	*18*
Panama	*18*
USA	*18*
South America	18
Ecuador	*18*
Peru	*18*
Bolivia	*20*
Argentina	*20*
Chile	*20*
Argentina - Patagonia	*21*
Asia	21
Thailand	*22*
Cambodia	*22*
Vietnam	*23*
China	*23*
Laos	*25*
Thailand	*25*
Malaysia	*26*
Singapore	*26*
Oceania	27
Australia	*27*

New Zealand	*28*
North America	28
USA- Alaska	*28*
Canada	*28*
West Coast	*30*
Across the USA	*32*
Asia	33
India	*33*
Part 2 - Planning - From Decision to Departure	**36**
CHAPTER 2 WHOSE IDEA WAS IT?	37
CHAPTER 3 HOW DID YOU GET STARTED?	41
What was the hardest part?	42
How did you finance the trip?	46
What was your daily budget?	47
What gear did you bring?	49
What was it like the day you left?	49
CHAPTER 4 WHAT WAS IT LIKE CHANGING YOUR LIFESTYLE?	53
The concept of time	54
Buying food at the market	56
Part 3 - On the Road	**58**
CHAPTER 5 WHAT DO YOU THINK ABOUT WHEN YOU'RE ON THE BIKE?	59
Mexico	60
Guatemala	61
Getting off the pity pot	61
Cambodia	63
USA - Impact of Economics	64
Political oppression	64
Tibetans - Impact of Religion	64
Hmong - Laos	65
CHAPTER 6 HOW DID PEOPLE REACT TO YOU?	67
Latin America	68
Laos	69
Westerners	69
Kindness of Strangers	70
Hobart, Tasmania	*70*
Sydney, Australia	*70*

Ruatoria, New Zealand	*70*
Cyclists	71
Laos	*71*
Australia	*71*
USA	*71*
CHAPTER 7 WERE YOU EVER SCARED?	**73**
Crossing the Border into Mexico	73
Tunnels	75
Guanajuato, Mexico	*75*
Dogs	78
Guns	79
Laos	*79*
Getting Arrested in China	80
CHAPTER 8 WHAT WAS IT LIKE GETTING VISAS AND CROSSING BORDERS?	**83**
Visas	83
Border Crossings	84
Peru/Bolivia	*84*
Thailand /Cambodia	*85*
Singapore	*87*
Part 4 - Stories from the Road	**88**
CHAPTER 9 WHAT WERE YOUR BEST BICYCLE RIDES?	**89**
Savannah Way	89
CHAPTER 10 WHAT WERE YOUR FAVORITE PLACES?	**99**
Palenque – Mexico	99
Angkor Wat – Cambodia	102
Machu Picchu – Peru	104
The Ups and Downs of Empires	105
CHAPTER 11 WHO ARE THE PEOPLE YOU REMEMBER MOST?	**107**
Maria in Guatemala	107
Lucho in Peru	109
David in Malaysia	110
CHAPTER 12 WHAT WERE YOUR FAVORITE PARTS OF THE JOURNEY?	**113**
Food	113
Favorite Festivals	114
Alms Luang Prabang	*114*

Festival Thai Sangkran	116
Fire-walking in Malaysia	116
Wildlife	119
Australia	120
Part 5 - Low Points & Lessons	**124**
CHAPTER 13 DID YOU GET SICK ON THE ROAD?	125
Parasites	126
Shingles	129
CHAPTER 14 WHY DID YOU STOP TRAVELING?	131
Australia	131
India	132
CHAPTER 15 LESSONS FROM THE ROAD	139
The Myth	140
Guatemala	140
Bolivia	142
I can is better than I can't	142
Ecuador	142
Pushing through difficult times	142
Vietnam	143
The benefits of forgiveness	143
Laos	145
The best gift of all - happiness	145
CHAPTER 16 END OF JOURNEY REFLECTIONS	147
Less is better	149
Health	150
Education	151
I didn't change, my perception did	152
EPILOGUE	153
FOOTNOTES	154
ABOUT THE AUTHOR	155

Prologue

Changing the course of one's life is sometimes the result of making a deliberate personal decision to live differently; sometimes it is by events, and other times it's by your association with others. Had it been left completely up to me, I would have been content to continue pursuing my American dream, the path I was already on. It would not have been by exploring the world from a bicycle.

I was the first woman in my family to get a college education and I had a professional, fulfilling career as a geologist. I was satisfied with the prospect of happily retiring at some point, content with my accomplishments, knowing I had exceeded all my life expectations. Instead, in 2002, I made a sharp detour and followed my husband, Tim, who pried me away from my comfortable western lifestyle to see the world.

In doing this, he opened a door that eventually changed my life forever. On March 30, 2002, we set off from our home in Prescott, Arizona for places unknown; our plan was to travel the world for seven years from our bicycles. It was never our goal to ride through as many countries as we could or to pedal a predetermined distance. Our goal was simply to not have a goal. Eight and a half years later, we had traveled over thirty thousand miles (forty-eight thousand kilometers) and visited twenty-three countries. Most importantly — as the saying goes — it wasn't the destination, but the journey along the way.

In the beginning, I had no intention of having a spiritual awakening, but rather I would explore the world, enjoy different foods, and experience different cultures while visiting some of the famous sites, such as Machu Piccu, the Great Wall of China, the Australian Outback, and others.

Many people ask, what was the hardest part of the trip? Without a doubt, it was the simple act of getting out the door. After that, everything fell into place and happened spontaneously. Along the way, we began to write and publish books about each segment of our expedition, based on my daily journals and his newsletters. When my travels ended I wrote about our nine-month excursion in China and published, *Finding Compassion in China: A Bicycle Journey into the Countryside*.

While working on that book, I realized I had missed the overall impact of my trip, so I shifted my focus from each segment to a view of the whole, which was all truly encompassing. I had made changes to every aspect of my life during those years. I went from being agnostic to Buddhist, and from being married to divorced. Of course, nothing changed overnight; sometimes things just happen.

While I struggled with how best to present the highs and lows of my travels, I realized I had already condensed the trip mentally when I had answered questions for various newspaper, podcast, and radio interviews. I decided that answering those prepared questions would be the best way to present my overall journey. I followed that up by sharing personal lessons I learned along the way, and, finally, reflecting on what I had observed in the world during that time.

In 2002, I stepped blindly through that opened door that led me to a world filled with amazing places and fascinating people. I will always be grateful for this gift and admire Tim's vision and courage to go against the grain and take me with him.

Acknowledgements

PODCASTS AND RADIO
Bicycle Touring Pro, Podcast, Darren Alff,
web site www.bicycletouringpro.com
Facebook https://www.facebook.com/bicycletouring

Gillian Ferris, KNAU/NPR Flagstaff, Arizona - Morning Edition,
web site http://knau.org/

Kansas Cyclist Podcast, Randy Rasha,
web site http://www.kansascyclist.com/

Roger Wendell, Denver Boulder Community Public Radio,
web site https://www.kgnu.org/

San Francisco BikeScape Podcast, Jon Winston,
web site http://www.bikescape.blogspot.com

Traveling Two Postcast, Andrew & Friedel Grant,
web site http://travellingtwo.com/
Facebook https://www.facebook.com/TravellingTwoBicycleTouring

INTERVIEWS AND PRESENTATIONS

The Path Less Pedaled, Laura Crawford and Russ Roca,
web site http://www.pathlesspedaled.com
Facebook https://www.facebook.com/pathlesspedaled
Presentation at Velo Cult, Portland Oregon.

Familyonbikes, Nancy Sathre-Vogel,
web site http://familyonbikes.org/
interview http://familyonbikes.org/blog/?s=cindie+cohagan&submit.x=6&submit.y=9
Facebook https://www.facebook.com/FamilyonBikes.org

Solo Female Cycling Around the World, Loretta Henderson,
web site http://www.skalatitude.com/
interview http://www.skalatitude.com/2011/10/we-want-freedom-in-interview-with-cindy.html
Facebook https://www.facebook.com/lorettahenderson333
twitter @skalatitude

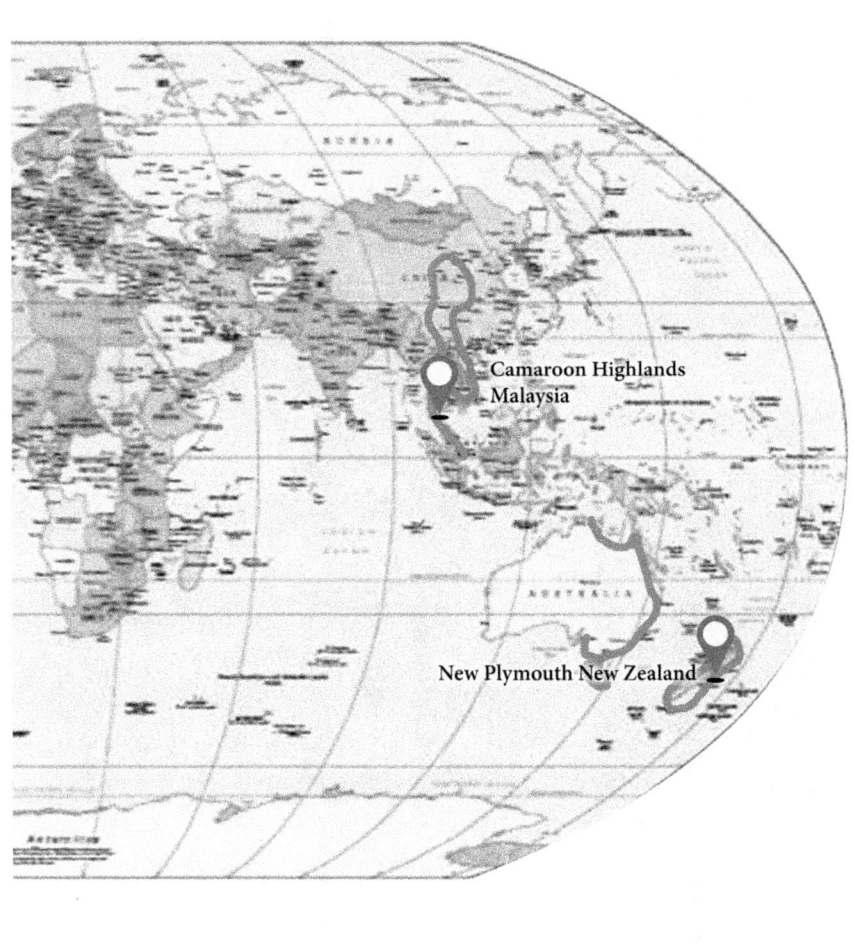

Part 1 - Introduction

Riding over Thompson Pass, Alaska, USA.

Chapter 1
Bicycling Thirty Thousand Miles through Twenty-Three Countries

It was January 2002 when we finally kick-started our maiden voyage, when my husband, Tim, and I took our first steps toward a life that would eventually take us around the world on bicycles. The subsequent eight and a half year journey began in our 1976 Ford Model C class RV.

We had packed two touring bikes and gear, and complete riding apparel. Since our plan included two more months of working, I brought a few work clothes, as well. Canned creamed corn, string beans and peas, all remnants of my overzealous bulk buying habit, moved from the kitchen cupboard to the RV pantry.

Five years of saving money, one year of downsizing, and six months of disconnecting delivered us to this point. Saving money was easier than I had thought; a low mortgage and both cars paid off reduced our monthly debt and increased our savings. My biannual work bonuses went straight into the travel fund. Downsizing, however, was harder than I expected; I was used to the habit of buying what I wanted when I wanted it. Throughout the planning years, I assessed every purchase. *Do I need this?* Most times the answer was no. Disconnecting was a downright pain. Changing bank accounts, closing credit cards, (offers from credit card companies increased when I did this) consolidating my retirement accounts, and finding a property manager for our house took more time than expected.

On our way to Mingus Mountain, our new residence in the Prescott National Forest, we stopped at a gas station on Robert Road. It had everything we needed – gasoline for the RV, propane for the fridge and heater, and snacks for me. Tim and I were still digesting our new sense of freedom when we parked our RV at a pump. Tim jumped out to fill up with gasoline. Seconds later, an old tan Chevy Nova pulled up to the pump next to us.

Out stepped a middle-aged driver with long brown hair and a tattoo of an eagle on his right forearm. Before he could even put the gas nozzle into his tank, I heard Tim say in an excited voice, "Hello. I am leaving on an around the world bicycle trip." To my surprise, the driver patiently stood next to Tim, listening intently to what he had to say.

Our home for two months before departure.

"Really," replied the man.

"Yes. We just moved out of our house in Prescott and into this RV. We're going to park in the Prescott National Forest tonight," Tim said enthusiastically.

"That's nice," the man said, as he finished pumping his gas and walked into the convenience store to pay.

By the time the man came out of the store, Tim had already moved our RV to the propane tank and finished filling it. I watched from the passenger seat as the man, instead of going back to his car, went directly over to Tim. In almost a whisper he said, "Aw, man. I understand you're down on your luck and don't have any money. You don't need to make up a story." He paused briefly and said, "I'll help you out. I paid for your propane."

Tim was stunned. All he could say was, "Wait! Wait!" The man put his hand up to signal Tim to stop talking and said, "I hope you have a nice day. Things will get better." Tim had no reply.

I tried to stay silent, but instead, I giggled. "That was a generous thing for him to do. Even if he didn't believe you," I said. The shocked expression on Tim's face was priceless. And he was speechless, a condition that rarely happens. In a heartbeat, his gratitude turned to anguish that the man didn't believe him. "It's all right Tim. Riding a bike around the world is hard to believe," I said.

I, on the other hand, couldn't stop giggling; mostly because of Tim's reaction and unrealistic expectation that people would believe he was riding his bike around the world. He would never be able to convince the man in the tan shirt of the truth; the truth was still too unbelievable.

Personally, I was thankful for the laugh; it relieved the tension that comes with stepping into the unknown. I was also grateful for his generosity and willingness to help out another person he perceived to be down on his luck. It reinforced my belief that people are good. I didn't know it at the time, but this was the beginning of being on the receiving end of a humbling amount of generosity.

THE TRIP

It was two months later, March 30, 2002, when we transitioned to traveling on touring bicycles. The lifestyle change was like stepping into a new pair of shoes that fit. The ease of my transition surprised both Tim and me. It tapped a part of me that had been dormant my entire life. I was a nomad who cherished the rhythm of the road and the opportunity to explore my surroundings.

From March 2002 until October 2010, we rode in twenty-three countries covering about 30,000 miles (48,000 kilometers) on four continents while writing and publishing three travel books.

I toured on a steel Bruce Gordon in North and South America, changed to a Koga-Myata aluminum bike for Southeast Asia, China, Australia, New Zealand and North America and finished with a steel Surly Long Haul Trucker for India.

We lived outdoors most of the time; our daily challenges were road conditions, seasons, and the weather. The world is not flat and not all roads are paved. We toured on unpaved or dirt roads when we had no choice. Wind direction made all the difference in how our day went. Headwinds slowed us down and even knocked me off my bike a few times. A tailwind was always welcomed and turned my two-wheeled vehicle into a sailboat. We didn't ride in the rain in North and South America because we didn't have fenders on our bikes. In Southeast Asia, we had to ride in the rain or not tour at all. We had to get used to what I eventually called a "plum rain," a slight but steady drizzle. We were at the mercy of hailstorms, thunderstorms, and hurricanes. Over time, we learned to read the weather better and, for the most part, avoided trouble. Occasionally, Mother Nature reminded us of her power, like the thunderstorm that hit us on a warm night in Nebraska when we got lazy and didn't stake down our tent.

The remote areas of Alaska, the American Southwest, Canada, the Tibetan area of the Himalayas and the Australian Outback (What Were Your Best Bicycle Rides? Chapter 9) were my favorite places to ride. We spent an extensive amount of time in Bariloche, Argentina; Cameroon Highlands, Malaysia; New Plymouth, New Zealand; Valdez, Alaska; and Batesville, Indiana writing and publishing our travel books.

My favorite places to visit were the Angkor Wat ruins in Siem Reap, Cambodia; Inca ruins of Machu Picchu near Aguas Calientes, Peru; Mayan ruins of Palenque in Chiapas, Mexico; the Perito Morano glacier in Patagonia, Argentina; and Port Arthur, Tasmania, Australia (What Were Your Favorite Places? Chapter 10).

Of the many festivals and religious rituals we encountered, the three that stand out the most for me are alms in Luang Phrabang, Laos, Sangkran in Thailand, and a fire-walking ceremony in Malaysia (What Were Your Favorite Parts of the Journey? Chapter 12).

When I look at a world map and reminisce about the places I have been, I smile because I am lucky. I am a wanderer who was given an opportunity to explore. In many ways, we weren't like other touring cyclists; rather than only riding, I spent weeks writing a journal, labeling photos, and working on taxes for our new publishing business. Changing hats from cyclist to traveler, to bean counter/tax accountant, to publisher kept me from ever getting bored.

THE CONTINENTS

North and Central America

Arizona

We navigated around Arizona for six weeks, (March 30 to May 13, 2002) and 700 miles (1,127 kilometers) gaining our cycling legs, finishing our hepatitis shots, and sifting through our still abundant gear prior to crossing the border into Mexico. Arizona proved to be a challenging place to start; the daily temperatures were above average (over 95°F, 35°C) in the desert areas near Phoenix and Tucson. We detoured to Portal, Arizona to hike and bird watch. We chose a small border crossing at Douglas/Agua Prieta to enter Mexico.

Mexico

We stepped across the Mexican border on May 13, 2002, stayed six months and rode 1,921 miles (3,090 kilometers). We bused from Cuauhtemoc to Zacatecas in northern Mexico, and Amecameca to Villa Hermosa in eastern Mexico. Our cycling route took us down the middle through the Sierra Madres of central Mexico and then through the states of Yucatan and Chiapas.

We attended Spanish school for nearly four weeks in Guanajuato located in central Mexico. It was here I discovered my fear of tunnels (Were You Ever Scared? Chapter 7). We were drawn to Aztec ruins of Teotihuacan in Mexico City, Olmec heads in the state of Tabasco, and Mayan ruins of Palenque in Chiapas. My desire to see antiquities and learn Spanish continued into Central America.

Guatemala

We arrived in Guatemala on December 2, 2002, stayed for thirty-five days, and rode 218 miles (351 kilometers). By this time, I had settled into the rhythm of riding daily and began to view my surroundings with more consideration rather than just observation. This led to a lesson that changed my life. I describe that process in What Do You Think About on the Bike? Chapter 5 and the lesson learned in Lessons from the Road Chapter 15.

Honduras

Riding from Guatemala to Honduras on a rainy day made it the muddiest border crossing. We stayed twenty-five days, rode 377 miles (607 kilometers), and took a detour to visit Parque Nacional Cero Azul Meambar cloud forest.

Nicaragua

Leaving Honduras was easy, entering Nicaragua was not. We didn't have the paperwork required for our bicycles; in the end our bikes were permitted to stay longer than we were. To avoid conflict, we left after twenty-five days, 293 miles (472 kilometers), and a week's stay at Ometepe, an island in the middle of Lake Nicaragua.

The island of Ometepe is the convergence of two volcanos, Volcano Conception and Volcano Maderas. Being in shape from cycling didn't seem to make a difference on the long trek to the summit and back of Volcano Maderas. My legs hurt for three days afterward.

Costa Rica

It was a pleasure to ride into Costa Rica on February 19, 2003. We stayed nearly two months and rode 296 miles (476 kilometers). When my twin sister, Cherie, and nephew, James, came to visit, we stayed at Rancho Mastatal, an environmental learning and sustainable living center, and Santa Elena, home to a Quaker community.

Panama

Visiting the Panama Canal was a highlight of our short five-day stay in Panama.

USA

From Panama we returned to Indiana for six and a half weeks prior to flying into Quito, Ecuador to start the South American leg of our tour. We purchased more supplies and packed our hiking gear to explore Ecuador by foot before starting our bicycle tour.

South America

Ecuador

To board our flight to Quito, Ecuador on June 4, 2003, we had to pay US$260 for our hiking and biking gear, and bicycles. It would have been more if Tim hadn't tipped the scales in our favor when they counted our total kilograms.

We remained in Ecuador for two months. The first three weeks we hiked around Banos, Ecuador and camped near Volcano Tungurahua. Our bike tour started in Quito and continued to the Peruvian border at Macara. Rather than ride along the mosquito-infested coast, we cycled 447 miles (720 kilometers) through the Andes. Staying above the malaria zone of 8,202 feet (2,500 meters) was better than taking a prophylactic. In the towns of Mocha and Columbe we stayed with Ecuadorian families. From the mountains of Ecuador we descended to the deserts of northern Peru.

Peru

We were in Peru from August to the end of October 2003, cycling 1,300 miles (2,092 kilometers) mostly through the Andes. Peru was a mix of fascinating people, health issues, numerous tunnels, Inca ruins, and high mountain passes.

In some of the northern Peruvian desert villages, the men were so aggressive I had to ride in front of Tim, instead of drafting behind him. Otherwise, the men yelled, sneered, or tried to grab me. As if to balance things out, we met two of the most memorable people of our trip within a week of each other.

Chino Moreno lives in Puente Chicama, a surfer town world renowned for the longest left hand curl. When conditions are right, an experienced surfer can ride a wave for 1.25 miles (over two kilometers). When the waves were in, the town turned into an instant surfer mecca, and when the seas were calm it was a ghost town. Surfers were now using the Internet to find the best waves in the world.

A couple of days later, we met Lucho, in Trujillo, who runs one of the most famous Casa de Cyclistas (Cyclist's House) in the world. (Who Are the People You Remember the Most? Chapter 11).

After Trujillo, we ascended back into the Andes through thirty-six tunnels along with a cyclist from Germany and stayed above 9,840 feet (3,000 meters) for nearly a month.

The pounding dirt roads (and lack of clean toilets) caused a painful bladder infection, forcing me off the bike for a few days, and eventually to a hospital in Puno.

While high in the Andes, Tim crashed at the top of a 6,500 foot (1,981 meters) descent. We stayed in Huanuco for a week while he recovered. Our fellow cyclist rode on; we stayed behind and, by chance, watched a peaceful protest at the square across from our hotel turn violent.

Near Pachapaqui, we climbed over a pass at 14,035 feet (4,278 meters), my personal best at the time. We wouldn't exceed that altitude until reaching the Tibetan area of Kham in the Himalayas.

To avoid unrest in the mountains and a long lonely stretch of Peruvian lowlands, we bused from La Oroya through Lima to Cusco. Cusco's many churches are built on top of old Incan temples. Viewing those churches, other Inca ruins, and visiting Machu Picchu kept us busy while we waited for a package from the USA. The border with Bolivia was closed by protests, as well. Our package didn't arrive before our visas expired, but at least the protests ended, the border opened, and we were allowed to enter Bolivia.

Bolivia

On November 1, 2003 we crossed the border from Peru to Bolivia; we could still see the barriers (now pushed to the side of the road) used to block vehicle traffic (What Was it Like Getting Visas and Border Crossings? Chapter 8). At least we were able to ride across the Salar de Uyuni, the largest salt flat in the world, with our friend from Munich, Germany.

The Salar was an adventure to traverse. Mostly because we didn't have a map, weren't sure if we had enough water, and Tim blew out the side of a tire in the middle of nowhere. Carrying a spare folding tire in his pannier was worth the weight; otherwise, the trip across the salt would have been a disaster. Still, we couldn't avoid trouble in Bolivia. Our ride (518 miles, 833 kilometers) was cut short by protests in Uyuni and we were lucky to catch a train to the border of Argentina after thirty-seven days in Bolivia.

Argentina

Argentina is a First World country with clean streets, healthy people, and good food. A welcomed change from the many months of hard traveling through Ecuador, Peru, and Bolivia. Crossing the border into Argentina on December 9, 2003 was easier than getting money from an ATM. We waited in a long line at the ATM and when we tried to withdraw money the machine malfunctioned. The receipts read, "Contact the Bank." And, "Didn't Dispense Money." On the third try, it dispensed the cash. When I reviewed my bank account, the Argentinian bank had withdrawn money from all three transactions. I disputed the error and got my money back.

Traveling down the east side of the Andes (445 miles, 716 kilometers), we visited national parks and camped with locals at the petrol (gas) stations. Cycling over the mountains to Chile through one tunnel and catching a ride through another was both heart-pounding and breathtaking. We had Aconcagua at 22,837 feet (6,961 meters), the highest mountain in the Americas, to view during the ride.

Chile

We cycled a short distance in Chile (361 miles, 581 kilometers) but I enjoyed the trout streams, volcanoes, and ferry rides through fjord country. We rode with a German woman until Tim had bike trouble and we had to get a new hub shipped from the USA. We traveled back over the Andes (not nearly as high as in the north) to Argentina.

Argentina - Patagonia

It was a short ride into Bariloche where we rented a car and explored southern Patagonia, backpacked for a week in Torres del Paine in Chile, and visited one of my favorite places, the Perito Moreno glacier, twice. We stayed in Bariloche for three months and settled into working on our first book – Tim writing and me keeping the author fed.

We returned to Indiana, USA to continue work on our project. We set a production deadline of October 28, 2004 for our first book, *The Road That Has No End: How We Traded Our Ordinary Lives for a Global Bicycle Touring Adventure*. Never having done anything like that before, I climbed a steep learning curve that drained every ounce of my energy. We made that deadline and sold our books at the Hilly Hundred, a large bike festival in Indiana, USA. At the time, self-published books were a novelty and our book sold well. It would take nearly four years before we finished our second book, about South America, *Down the Road in South America, A Bicycle Tour Through Poverty and Paradise*.

With the first book finished, we had a month to prepare for the next leg of our cycling expedition.

Asia

We landed in Thailand and remained in Asia for twenty-two months, cycling 7,880 miles (12,682 kilometers) through seven countries. Over a year in the communist countries of China, Vietnam, and Laos altered my views on communism. I came away with the impression that it is all about what is good for the masses and not the individual. Severe political, religious, and cultural oppression (What Did You Think About on The Bike? Chapter 5) was common in all three countries.

Even though some areas of Southeast Asia had experienced famine and continued to eat spiders, maggots, and sometimes dogs, the local food was the best in the world.

Buddhism, Hinduism, and Islam religions dominate the region. The introduction to Buddhism would have a lasting effect on me.

Thailand

Landing in Bangkok, Thailand, on November 22, 2004, was a thrill. I was ecstatic to be on the road again after taking nearly nine months off to write and publish our first book. Starting again in Asia at the end of 2004 was quite similar to leaving our front door in 2002. Both times we had new bikes, were overloaded with gear, were out of shape, had an escort out of town, and Tim got a flat on the first day.

Many smiles, 339 miles (546 kilometers) and twenty-four days later, we left easy-going Thailand behind and crossed the border into Cambodia.

Cambodia

Contrary to my initial expectations of finding a downtrodden group of people, Cambodians were young, optimistic, and endearing.

In 2004, the road between Aranyaprathet, Thailand and Siem Reap, Cambodia was a bumpy dust bowl. So dusty, face masks were mandatory. Riding into the upscale tourist town of Siem Reap, with five-star accommodations, I noticed a number of nonprofit organizations (NGOs) were roughing it and had their headquarters there. A week at Angkor Wat, the world's largest religious monument, wasn't long enough for me. Traveling from Siem Reap to Phnom Penh with two Canadian cyclists maximized our speed.

In the remote town of Kompong Thnor, we heard on BBC radio about the tsunami that hit the west coast of Thailand on Boxing Day (December 26). No one knew the full extent of the Boxing Day tsunami until days later. First reports put the casualties at 11,000 people; the death toll grew to over 230,000 people in Indonesia, Thailand, Malaysia, Bangladesh, Sri Lanka, Maldives, and India. We would see that destruction on Thailand's west coast a year later.

A visit to the Killing Fields and Tuol Sleng prison where Pol Pot and the Khmer Rouge tortured, imprisoned, and executed thousands of people will haunt me for the rest of my life. I still remember the old woman in Phnom Penh whose face was still frozen in trauma. *How can people be so cruel?* This is the question that continues to echo in my mind.

Ruins at Ta Prohm, Angkor Wat, Cambodia.

An extended stay in Phnom Penh waiting for new ATM cards proved to be futile. With our thirty-day visas about to expire, we pushed on over dirt roads and through dusty air into Vietnam. In thirty days we had cycled 501 miles (806 kilometers).

Vietnam

In Vietnam, my grim expectations were extinguished again. Worrying that locals wouldn't like Americans was a waste of energy. Except for the drunk who hit me, I experienced a forgiving and tenacious people who bargained hard with foreigners in northern and southern Vietnam.

The government was another story. I had to get used to someone peering over my shoulder and reading my computer screen at the Internet cafés. We met a few individuals from the south who ended up in re-education camps.

The cleaning crew robbed our room at Buon Ma Thuot while we were at lunch. It was Tet (Chinese New Year) so the police were hard to locate, but when they finally arrived, they helped more than I could have imagined. The next morning, I found most of our money had been pushed under the door during the night. The police returned, asked how we were doing, and were not surprised most of our money reappeared. They insisted we not pay for our room and we left Buon Ma Thout quickly.

Not long after, in the town of Peliku, the police called our room; they wanted to know our itinerary and when we told them we were going west they explained that area was closed to foreigners. The only way we could leave town was back to the coast. We didn't have an escort out of town, however, I had the distinct feeling we were being watched. This kind of treatment didn't change when we got to China, it got worse.

Nearly three months and 973 miles (1,565 kilometers) later we entered China.

China

Nine months and 3,880 miles (6,244 kilometers) of cycling in China were enough for me in some ways (I was tired of the government's antics) but not enough in others (so many places to explore and cultures to see).

We started out on the wrong foot by getting arrested thirteen days into the country (Were You Ever Scared? Chapter 7). It opened my eyes to the constant surveillance techniques used by the government on both foreigners and locals. It also put traveling into perspective, hearing that people went to prison for holding up a sign in protest, made seeing the Great Wall of China feel like a trivial desire. Balancing out the government's paranoia were the trusting and welcoming gestures we received from the locals.

Extending our ninety-day tourist visas was difficult; we were turned down twice and we suspected it was due to having been arrested. We had seen a small part of China in a little over two months and we both wanted to see more. We hopped a train to Beijing to meet my Aunt Joan and while there purchased six-month business visas.

Visas in hand, we set off to explore more of China starting with Inner Mongolia. Riding from the south (Han Chinese) to the north side (Mongolian) of the Great Wall was like going through a border check. Language, food, and culture were all different on the other side. The Mongolians have different mannerisms than the Chinese and enjoyed touching us, our bikes, and all our gear.

As a rule, foreigners are not allowed to stay with locals or at small guesthouses. However, in Inner Mongolia we had no choice but to stay in a small guesthouse. We rolled our bikes into the front room and the entire town followed us in, filling the small apartment to standing room only.

From Inner Mongolia we cycled to Xian to examine the Terracotta Warriors. While there, we heard about Hurricane Katrina wiping out New Orleans. I was saddened but not surprised by the destruction and couldn't believe how disorganized my country appeared.

From Xian we took the train to Chengdu, visited the Chengdu Research Base of Giant Panda Breeding and the tea houses around town. We set off for the Tibetan area with a French cyclist and we rode together for a week. Cycling in Kham was physically challenging; we traversed the highest pass of the trip and my new personal best at around 17,056 feet (5,199 meters).

Learning more about Tibetan Buddhism by visiting monasteries, turning prayer wheels, and watching Tibetans incorporate every aspect of Buddhism into their daily life sparked an interest in me that grew with time. Visiting ethnic minorities, including Tibetans at high altitude in Sichuan province, and the Yi, Bai, and Naxi at lower altitudes in Yunnan province, revealed the diversity of China. It was in those areas the Han Chinese men were encouraged to move for work and to marry minority women they could have more than one child with.

It wasn't until I wrote *Finding Compassion in China: A Bicycle Journey into the Countryside* that I realized we traveled mostly in the minority areas.

Laos

After nine long months in China, it felt like we returned to the tourist zone on December 25, 2005, when we entered Laos. In thirty days, we traveled 469 miles (756 kilometers) from the Chinese to the Thai border with plenty of hills in between. Hmong hill tribes, ancient tea plantations, bad Chinese drivers, a dilapidated American military base, hundreds of touring cyclists, and partying natives filled our days in Laos. The young boys welcomed us with their sling shots while some of the men toted AK-47s.

Luang Prabang is an ancient city located in the middle of the country at the confluence of the Nam Khan and Mekong rivers. One of the more popular routes in *Lonely Planet Cycling Vietnam, Laos & Cambodia* starts from Luang Prabang and goes to Vientiane, the capital of Laos located along the border with Thailand. It was on this section of the road we met most touring cyclists.

Thailand

Fourteen months after leaving Thailand, we returned to cycle its length (1,192 miles, 1,918 kilometers). Upon returning to Bangkok, we had made a full circle through Asia. This may not sound like much, but most touring cyclists don't ride in loops, they ride in a straight line from point A to point B.

Fifteen months after the Boxing Day tsunami hit the western coast of Thailand, we were sitting in a guesthouse at Ban Niang Beach, one of the hardest hit areas in Thailand. I heard some amazing stories, like the British girl who had studied tsunamis in school and ran up and down the beach warning people a wave was coming. She saved many lives that day. We also saw the patrol boat that was guarding the king's grandson; it was deposited 0.625 miles (over one kilometer) inland and left as a memorial to all the people who lost their lives that day, including the king's grandson.

A quick trip into Myanmar to extend our visas another thirty days, so we could ride to the border of Malaysia, was surreal (a short boat ride to a five-star hotel) and expensive.

Malaysia

Before arriving in Malaysia in April 2006, I knew very little about it except that it is a Muslim country, once included in the British Empire. We were pleasantly surprised by the number of tourist sites, religious ceremonies, and annual events we saw, including a fire-walking ceremony (What Were Your Favorite Parts of the Journey? Chapter 12), a Chinese opera, a Buddhist temple, including a life size rendition of hell (eerily similar to the Christian's Judgment Day), a Chinese funeral, Ghost Month festivities, a Tamil Indian wedding, and a standing on a sword ceremony.

With all these activities, working on an audiobook, and web site, we didn't ride much (562 miles, 904 kilometers) in the four and a half months we spent in Malaysia.

Once we left our ten-week perch in the Cameroon Highlands, we stayed with our friend David (Who Do You Remember the Most? Chapter 11). He took us on day rides around Purit Buntar exploring the nearby Muslim communities, viewing the monitor lizards (that looked like they had stepped out of the dinosaur era), and visiting the Chinese bird nest factories. The Chinese eat and drink the strangest things, such as bird nest soup or bird nest drink. According to Wikipedia, most nests are built during the breeding season by the male swiftlet over a period of thirty-five days.

Good food, friendly people, diverse cultures, and religions with a First World infrastructure (we could drink the water out of the tap) puts Malaysia high on my list to return to.

Singapore

We weren't done being detained by police in Asia. Just like the first time, we didn't know we were doing anything wrong. Singapore is an island and to get there we had to cross a bridge. We chose the closest bridge to us, called the Second Link. It's legal for a cyclist to cross the bridge in Malaysia but not in Singapore. What is a cyclist to do, but ride right into an unknown trap (What was it Like Getting Visas and Border Crossings? Chapter 8)?

We spent our short stay in Singapore visiting our friend Andy (who cycled from England to Singapore), eating out, and shopping for what we needed for Australia. We even gave our bikes a bath in our hotel shower. Australian immigration is known for checking for dirt on bikes coming into Australia. If the bike is dirty, it's quarantined and cleaned at the owner's expense.

Oceania

Australia

It took planning and persistence to get one-year tourist visas for Australia. Our biggest obstacle came out of nowhere. Australia immigration requires a chest X-ray from travelers who have been to areas with high tuberculosis (TB) rates like Mexico, China, and Laos. Tim's chest X-ray showed the classic signs of TB. He was required to submit a sputum sample each day at the hospital for three days in a row; the results came back negative. Australia let us in on the condition he get tested again when we landed. Tim never tested positive.

It's hard to describe what it's like to go from a country where I don't understand what everyone is saying to a country that speaks my native tongue. At first my brain was overloaded with so much information, I searched for an off switch and didn't find one.

Landing in Adelaide (a city in South Australia) in September 2006 and traveling in a counterclockwise direction, we explored the continent. A six-week tour of the island of Tasmania, inland from Melbourne to Canberra and up to Cairns we continued toward Katherine, then out to Kakadu National Park, cycling 4,740 miles (7,628 kilometers).

Australia is a bird watcher's and animal lover's paradise. I searched for wildlife with a pair of binoculars daily and was rewarded with seeing the most amazing creatures. The platypus, echidna, wombat, and kangaroo are all animals straight out of a children's book. My fondest memory of Australia is waking to the smell of gum (eucalyptus) trees and the sound of the Laughing Kookaburra, a relative of the kingfisher.

We stayed with friends of friends, met people who followed us on the Internet, camped in a tent ninety percent of the time, had family come to visit us, splurged on seeing the Great Barrier Reef (it was well worth it), and best of all, we rode across the top of Australia on the Savannah Way

(What Were Your Best Bicycle Rides? Chapter 9).

New Zealand

House sitting in Auckland gave us a chance to catch up on bike work and assess our health. Through most of Australia, Tim hadn't felt well. A trip to a doctor specializing in travel illnesses revealed his problem. He had a parasite and it probably had hitched a ride all the way from Vietnam or China (Did You Get Sick on the Road? Chapter 13).

We stayed close to two months in New Plymouth with a fellow cyclist, working on our book about South America. During nine months in New Zealand we rode 950 miles (1,529 kilometers) on the north and south islands.

I experienced my first earthquake, dragged Tim to the tip of the south island to see penguins, and met a beekeeper who showed me where the queen bee lives. Toward the end of our tour, we concentrated on getting rid of a parasite and finishing a book we had been working on for the last four years.

North America

USA- Alaska

On May 2, 2008 we arrived in Valdez, Alaska. Contrary to what most people think, Valdez is not where the Exxon Valdez oil spill occurred. The tanker ran aground in Prince William Sound, Alaska, on March 24, 1989, seventy miles (113 kilometers) from the Port of Valdez. Besides visiting my family, hiking Keystone Canyon, watching avalanches descend to the canyon floor, we finished our second book.

Returning to the USA meant riding on the right side of the road again, not an easy task after twenty-eight months of riding on the left. Habits are hard to change and at the first few intersections I was confused on which side of the road to ride. I was lucky to be in a small town where the drivers were forgiving.

Alaska's pristine wilderness, moose, grizzlies (a few bushes I thought were grizzlies), raspberries, salmon berries, and a handful of colorful characters (independent individuals with a flair for hunting, fishing, and prospecting) dominated the 410 miles (660 kilometers) we cycled.

Canada

Some days were full of obstacles and riding into Canada was one of those days. The last fifteen miles (twenty-four kilometers) in Alaska I was stuck in a low gear on flat terrain. The relatively new cable to my front derailleur broke, leaving me with no way to shift from one chain ring to the next. The chain dropped to the smallest ring forcing me to spin at a high rate; I felt like I was running in place. Meanwhile, Tim got a flat tire. I didn't mind because I watched a moose play in a nearby water hole while he changed it.

Ah, immigration at last. This should be easy. It wasn't. The customs official skimmed through my very full passport and began her interrogation. "Where have you been the last year?"

"Let's see. Australia, New Zealand, and Alaska (as if it was its own country)," I said.

She flipped through a few more pages of my passport studying each entry and exit stamp and said, "Why have you gone to all these other countries, like China?"

"We are bike tourists and travel writers," I said hesitantly, my new profession hadn't sunk in yet.

She looked at Tim to my right and said, "Give me his passport."

I handed over Tim's passport. I couldn't believe she was comparing my passport with his. For some reason, this made me panic and I volunteered, "I am the publisher and he is the author."

Still scrutinizing our passports, she replied with an "Uh huh" in a "I don't believe you" tone. She held Tim's passport up and I could see her eyes travel from Tim's passport photo to Tim.

Oh dear, this could be a problem. Tim had changed. In the photo he was clean shaven with short hair. Now, he looked more like an Alaskan, long wavy hair to his shoulders and a scruffy beard. Time was ticking and she was in no rush to let us pass through. Then what I was hoping for happened; she handed back both passports and said, "Welcome to Canada."

Whew. We pedaled to the nearest town and set up camp.

It was a rainy summer that year (2008), dodging thunderstorm cells was a dance we practiced every day. One particular day I wasn't feeling well: feverish, achy, maybe the flu. I thought a bump on my lower back was a spider bite. Tired and with no place to go, I rolled out my sleeping pad and took a nap on a picnic table while Tim sat nearby. Very odd behavior for me. My "spider bite" turned out to be shingles (Did You Get Sick on the Road? Chapter 13).

The next 1,055 miles (1,698 kilometers) through Canada were a blur. I do remember the beautiful scenery kept my mind off my pain. The terrain was relatively flat and, when it wasn't, my legs felt like lead, my heart raced, and the pain in my back – now present all the time – hurt more.

Constant rain didn't help my condition; we pushed on down the Cassier Highway, camping and eating wild berries (salmon, raspberry, saskatoon, and strawberries were the ones I would pick) while on high alert for bears. We saw eleven bears in Canada, not all of them saw us, however, I am sure they heard us. To ensure we never startled a bear while we were riding, Tim blared Metallica all the way down the Cassier Highway. It worked. We never startled a bear.

Near Terrance, Canada, we met a mushroom picker who was setting up camp for the season. He invited us in; we declined because we had to push on to Prince Rupert. Later, caught in a torrential downpour, we took cover at the mushroom picker's camp. We spent the next three days learning how to pick mushrooms, visited a First Nation settlement with a row of totem poles, and ventured into town for a trip to the grocery store.

The ferry ride from Prince Rupert to Port Hardy on Victoria Island was enjoyable especially when the Orca whale pod came to visit our boat. I was looking forward to returning to my home country and seeing what had changed over the last six and a half years.

West Coast

Going home to the USA was easy (I felt welcomed by immigration) and at the same time unsettling (I felt like I was in a foreign country). I felt out of sync with Americans. Technology had passed us by; we were at a loss without a phone.

The number of fellow Americans who took us in for a night or two was numerous. Being an election year (2008), people defined themselves as a Democrat or a Republican. I identify myself as an Independent, which made it easier to interact with both sides. That was how my country appeared to me, divided on every issue. You are either with me or against me echoed from both sides. Where had compromise, agree to disagree, and everyone is entitled to their own opinion gone? Fear had taken over; I was sad to see the state of my country.

Seventeen days after we returned home, the stock market crashed. We never experienced the heyday of the financial bubble, we only experienced the crash.

We carried on, pedaled 1,800 miles (2,897 kilometers) down the undulating west coast from Washington state to Ventura, California. Gasoline, at over four US dollars a gallon, sent Americans into a tailspin and onto their bikes. Our fellow bike tourists were young; we were old enough to be their parents. I didn't mind. They balanced out all the gasoline-burning machines that my generation owned.

Every hiker/biker campsite in a state or national park was occupied with cyclists in Washington and Oregon and a lot of homeless in California (where the weather is better).

Northern California, home of the giant redwoods, is a special place even though only two percent of the once grand forest remains. The groves we rode through were preserved for future generations, not by our park system, but by a group of people from San Francisco who pooled their money and bought large tracks of the redwoods in the 1920s. I am grateful to these true visionaries.

In San Francisco, we met a few members of Critical Mass (a group of cyclists who take to the streets in large numbers) who helped transform the city into a cycling mecca.

November 2008, we took a train from Ventura, California to Tucson, Arizona, stayed with friends in Tucson and sold books at El Tour de Tucson, a perimeter (around Tucson) ride attended by more than 4,000 cyclists. We took three months off in Yuma, Arizona, along with the rest of the snowbirds, sold books, learned Tai Chi, and rode with the bike club when we could.

We were the youngsters in this group of retirees. I learned a few lessons that winter and one being, some people grow old gracefully, some don't. Some people have an easy life, some don't. How one's retirement goes is an accumulation of one's life decisions. Regardless of what I do in my future, I will be happy in my retirement.

While in Yuma, thoughts of stopping and returning to work swirled around my head. If I could have gotten a job, I would have gone back to work. However, I was in the same boat as many Americans, no job. Financially, we were not in debt and that gave us a lot of freedom. It was time to write another book, which was a better alternative than what most Americans had. But first, a trip across the USA.

Across the USA

Leaving Yuma, we were out of shape and our bikes overloaded with food. Some things never change. This time it took my body longer to get used to going from Tai Chi three days a week to riding hours in a day. It was early March 2009, a good time to be camping in the desert; I loved the wildlife and wildflowers that were abundant that time of year.

We didn't ride directly to Prescott. Instead, we toured southern Arizona to Phoenix, and into Prescott the back way, through Congress, Yarnell, and then Wilhoit.

As we rode into Wilhoit, our friends, Marcie and Tom, stopped to say hello. It was good to see familiar faces. She assured me that dinner at Jim and Karen's would be ready for us when we got to Prescott.

All we had was one last push. It was amazing my legs knew exactly where I was; I knew every turn and hill. The hills weren't as bad as I remembered. When we reached the top of the pass, a place we used to stop on our club rides, we paused. Back then, it was a dense pine forest, now it was bare of trees. The Indian fire of 2002 wiped out the ponderosa pine stand there. As I reached back in my memory to what it used to be like, I was saddened by the absence of those grand trees.

Seven years and twelve days after leaving the Court House Square, we returned to Prescott from our around-the-world tour. In my heart, I was ready to finish, but reality was different. We were just passing through, not staying. I had an urge to turn up Copper Basin Road, back to my home, but I couldn't, because our house was occupied by renters. I had to follow a different path, one that led me away from what I thought was home.

It wasn't all bad; we were better off than most. We were still free to roam and took the opportunity to bike tour in America.

Seeing the Grand Canyon again reminded me why I love geology. Exploring the rest of Arizona, Utah, and Colorado was delightful. Once we got to the bread basket of America, things changed. There seemed to be friction between the cyclists and the locals, not everywhere, just certain places.

We were in time for RAGBRAI (Register's Annual Great Bicycle Ride Across Iowa), and we joined Team Roadshow for the event. We crossed Iowa with carnies (employees of a traveling amusement show) and I loved it. We rode the first day of RAGBRAI with thousands of other cyclists. I heard a woman ask her riding companion, "How do I stop the bike?" and I happily volunteered to be part of the bus crew. Besides, Tim and I could ride all the time, while the group of jugglers and unicycle riders were professors and engineers who worked hard to get that time off.

For seven days, Tim drove the vegetable-oil-burning bus that smelt like French fries as we cruised down the road. I picked out the campsite, and the rest of the crew organized camp. Then we waited for the riders to come in from the seventy- to ninety-mile (113 to 145 kilometers) ride.

After RAGBRAI, we returned to our Indiana home base for a short time, rode around Lake Ontario on Canada's side, continued on the Erie Canal tow path to meet a friend in Albany, New York.

Visiting family in Connecticut, riding my loaded touring bike in Manhattan, and visiting Pennsylvania Dutch/Amish country were highlights. Four days at Gettysburg and a visit to Washington, D.C. ended our USA tour. Our American tour from March to October 2009, including book presentations in Nebraska, Iowa, Indiana, and Connecticut, was around 2,450 miles (3,943 kilometers).

From Washington DC, we returned to our Indiana home base for the next eight months to write and publish our third book, *Down the Road in Thailand, Cambodia, and Vietnam: A Bicycle Tour Through War, Genocide and Forgiveness.*

Asia

India

We fell behind schedule on publishing our book and arrived in India three months later than expected. On April 30, 2010 we landed in Delhi and I was sick in bed for the next five days. Backpackers call it "Delhi Belly." I call it a bacterial infection. It was too close to the beginning of monsoon season to be touring in the Himalayas, where we planned to start our tour. After much debate and political unrest in Darjeeling, we settled on McLeod Ganj (also known as Upper Dharamsala), to wait out the rain. I was exhausted from publishing a book and I welcomed the opportunity to do yoga, hike, and relax in the privacy of my own room. I was also looking forward to attending a teaching by His Holiness The Dalai Lama because McLeod Ganj is his home in exile. During our stay, my interest in Buddhism waxed while my desire to continue bike touring waned. I was physically out of shape again. I knew what it would take to get my fitness back and I dreaded the process.

In September 2010, we cycled 157 miles (253 kilometers) from McLeod Ganj to Tso Pema, a small Tibetan Buddhist community. I returned to McLeod Ganj one week later, my travels were over (Why Did You Stop Traveling? Chapter 14).

Three years later, I am still in India finishing this book, wondering what the next chapter in my life will be.

A stopover at the Grand Canyon, Arizona, USA.

Part 2 - Planning - From Decision to Departure

Dreaming of a tropical vacation, beach at Manuel Antonio National Park, Costa Rica.

Chapter 2
Whose Idea Was It?

Traveling around the world by bicycle was Tim's aspiration; it was on his mind from the moment I met him. Maybe that's why I didn't take him seriously and thought he was a dreamer not a doer. That notion changed two years later when he was still telling everyone in our bike club about his plan to become a full-time bicycle tourist. As the president of the club, Tim usually attended every ride either mountain or road, wrote the monthly newsletter, and welcomed every new rider. Along with that initiation, he always told a new cyclist, "I am going on an around-the-world bicycle tour." Without fail, they would ask me if his bold announcement was true. At the time, it looked like an impossible undertaking to me, so when pressed, I always answered vaguely, "I don't know."

As far-fetched as his plan sounded, it captured my attention from the beginning. Curiosity about other countries and cultures had already pushed me out the door to Central America, Europe, Asia, and the Caribbean. My own desires to explore more of the world were rekindled by Tim's tenacious hold on his dream. Then I would come to my senses and realize that traveling the world by bicycle was an unlikely endeavor for many reasons.

I was concerned with costs, whether I could do it physically, and what I would be leaving behind. My previous travels had cost more money than Tim wanted to spend on this trip. I really became skeptical when he said we could travel on thirty US dollars a day for two of us. As long as we continued to save money, my concerns with costs were being addressed. Physically, I felt old already; I was nearly forty and out of shape. Lastly, I had a good job that I loved, even if it was wearing me out.

I had always considered myself healthy. I assumed this because I could eat whatever I wanted and never gained weight. I often ate macaroni and cheese for breakfast and a big Slurpee and a chilli dog from Sonic for lunch. Fast foods were a favorite of mine – it was fast, filling, and I could eat it in the car while on the job.

The illusion that I was healthy because I was thin and I rode a bicycle once in awhile was shattered when I was diagnosed with hypoglycemia, a precursor to diabetes. Hypoglycemia is an overproduction of insulin that causes a rapid drop in blood sugar levels. My mood swings, insomnia, and extra rolls around my middle (these were new) were a direct result of eating the wrong food, drinking alcohol, and having a stressful lifestyle.

My body was telling me I could no longer deal with poor eating habits and stress. I had to change my diet and fast. Out were bread, pasta, Pierogi (Polish dumplings), egg mcmuffins, hot dogs, and macaroni and cheese (I missed this one the most). In were oatmeal, apples, lettuce, tomatoes, meat in moderation, and anything I could buy at the weekly farmers market. Rather than eat three meals a day, I changed to five meals a day. Instead of fast food, I brought nuts, granola bars, cheese, apples, and beef jerky to work.

I never went anywhere without food; I had food in my car, in my desk, and in my pocket. The guys at work noticed the change and my new nickname became "chuck wagon." I didn't mind, it was better than some of the other nicknames I heard. Every time I felt my blood sugar drop, I ate something. It took months for my blood sugar to stabilize.

Along with changes in eating habits, I had to reduce my stress. I tried to increase my exercise. I rode with the bike club as often as I could. The club was mostly men with a few women who showed up daily. I rode with the women; they were always supportive and never teased me about falling off my mountain bike so easily. I wanted to get in shape. It was a two-steps-forward and one-backward process. Every time I reached a decent fitness level, I was called away on a job. I soon realized getting healthy was a three-part process: changing my eating habits, increasing my exercise, and reducing my stress. I could work on the first step most of the time but I wasn't successful in regulating my exercise or reducing my job stress.

I worked as a geologist for a small environmental consulting firm and my boss was one of the best advisors in the business. My responsibilities included long hours (eighty to one hundred hours a week) in the field, drilling wells, performing water quantity (availability) testing, and collecting water for quality (chemical) analysis. I learned a lot, it was great for my paycheck (and savings), but not my health. Whenever I was asked to go on a job, wherever it might be, I always said, "Yes." Even if it started on the weekend I was planning a bike trip. In the big picture, I was spending more time working than anything else, and through my lifestyle analysis, I began to feel like I was married to my job.

As my examination continued, it led me to questions. *What is it for? What am I working for?* My puzzled answer surprised me. *I don't know.* My career was established, I already lived in a modest home, owned my truck, and had all the bicycles I wanted (three: an around town bike, a mountain bike, and a road bike).

I wasn't saving for my child's college education because I didn't have any children. I observed the people closest to me who didn't have children. There were two differences between us – they had bigger houses and newer cars. When it struck me my future was the same, I felt like I had been hit by a Mack truck. I was shaken. *Is that it? Is that all I get for working long hours for the next twenty years, a bigger house and nicer cars?*

Holy cow! I was working to accumulate more material possessions. *Do I really need more?* My house already overflowed with whatever I wanted. My truck was old, but it still worked. *Do I want a new one? Well, yeah. Do I want to work for a minimum of three years of auto payments so I could have a new 4 X 4? No.* I suddenly felt my life was dedicated to using and consuming possessions.

My mind was made up in an instant. I didn't want to stay so I could buy a bigger house and a newer car. It was time to leave my comfortable western lifestyle and take a chance on bicycling around the world. This change in perception served to confirm that I wasn't leaving anything behind that I couldn't live without. I began to consider the benefits of changing my life.

I knew if I didn't do something about my health I would be miserable in my old age or shorten my life. I enjoyed life and wanted to be healthy. Looking around me I saw how unhealthy most people looked and I didn't want to join them. Working all those extra hours was shortening my life rather than enhancing it.

I didn't have children and was past the point of having them. I didn't have the responsibilities that most women have; I was free to roam.

The tipping point was pondering the future and contemplating what it would be like in twenty years. I knew I would regret having missed this opportunity.

Cindie Cohagan

Riding toward Volcano Llaima, Chile.

Chapter 3
How Did You Get Started?

Our camp site for a night - a bus stop in Guatemala.

During those saving money years, I fluctuated between periods of doubt and enthusiasm. I had many doubts. I worried about how vulnerable I would be, not just to the elements, but to dangerous people and lawless places. On the bike, we couldn't escape from a threatening situation quickly, like being robbed or getting caught in bad weather.

I pondered, *where will I sleep at night?* I assumed in a campground or in the forest. I never considered in a bus stop in Guatemala, a coffee plantation in Vietnam or near crocodile-infested waters in Australia.

And where will I find a bathroom? I wasn't the only one wondering where I would find a toilet. It was the first question a nine-year-old girl, in my nephew's classroom, asked me after my presentation about my upcoming trip. I quickly answered, "At the gas station." In reality, it was usually behind a bush, in a field, and a couple of times behind an umbrella.

At my high points, I dreamed about visiting Inca ruins in South America, eating Mexican and Thai foods, and riding my bicycle all day. I also thought, *I will have time to learn Spanish, exercise more and eat healthy.*

I never immersed myself in any language, definitely exercised more, and didn't always eat as healthy as I wanted.

Tim and I had many discussions about our future travels. One afternoon, Tim announced, "We will be traveling based on the weather."

"You mean we'll be like snowbirds and head south for the winter?" I asked.

"That's right."

What a fascinating idea. Traveling based on the weather and climate, not at the convenience of my work schedule or a cheap plane ticket. While this sounded appealing when I thought of warm weather and sunshine, I knew from working outdoors, weather is rarely comfortable all the time.

"Hey! What happens if it rains?" I said rather loudly because Tim was walking away into the kitchen.

"Don't worry. We will be carrying a tent," he called back confidently.

"That doesn't make me feel any better," I replied.

"If it rains, we will get a hotel room. But, if we aren't near a hotel when it rains, we can put up the tent."

"So you're saying we will get a hotel room if it rains?" I repeated.

"Yes, if we can," he answered.

With my worries about the weather pacified, I moved on to more pressing questions.

"What happens if we get robbed?" I asked.

"Don't worry! We won't be traveling in tourist areas too much."

"What do you mean by that?" I asked.

"Well, tourists are like deer and thieves are like hunters. Where the deer play the hunters go to hunt."

"What does that mean?" I asked.

"If we stay out of the tourist areas, we probably won't get robbed," he explained.

I could see the logic in his thinking, but I was still nervous about getting robbed and responded with a feeble, "OK." *I will have to trust that things will be okay.*

WHAT WAS THE HARDEST PART?

Without a doubt the hardest part of the trip was getting out the door.

Without realizing it, we had become tied to our jobs and home by material belongings. I was working to pay for my house, car, bikes, and trips to Starbucks. I looked around at all my possessions and realized I wasn't leaving until I sold, stored, or gave away every item I owned. A task that required more time and thought than I could give. Consequently, it was put off until the eleventh hour.

Reviewing what I owned was an excursion into what used to be a necessity or an entitlement. Mounds of excess collected in my closet and in the house in general. I hadn't taken a hard look into my lifestyle since I left college seventeen years earlier.

Detaching from everything I had worked so long to acquire wasn't easy. I was an accumulator, and accumulated the oddest things such as shirts, socks, and all kinds of bed sheets. Over seventy-five shirts, at least one hundred pairs of socks, and enough bed sheets to stock a motel filled my closet.

I had an endless supply of shirts including dress shirts, T-shirts, bike shirts, cleaning shirts, hiking shirts, shirts to wear out to a restaurant, and shirts to wear to work. A shirt for every occasion hung in my closet and if an occasion came around that I didn't have a shirt for, I went shopping. I found a few shirts that still had tags on them or had been worn only once. I had business suits and professional clothing that didn't fit anymore crammed in the back of my closet. This outfit I bought for that meeting with the EPA (Environmental Protection Agency), as if clothes defined my career.

Socks for every occasion were thrown in dresser drawers and tubs. When I started sorting through them it seemed I had more singles than pairs. Heck, I might find the other mate, the union between the lost pair would be monumental and I couldn't deny myself of that wonderful moment. Instead, I had a drawer full of single socks that were of no use to anyone. *Why am I holding on to these unmatched socks?* I tossed every sock without a mate in the garbage.

I still had a good amount of business clothes left in my closet that were too small for me. Rather than sell them, I donated them to the women's shelter down the street. I still remember the expression on the woman's face when I gave her six business suits with matching shoes and accessories. Her mouth hung open for a moment before she quickly gathered her composure and said, "I know someone who is doing an interview this week and could use one of these outfits."

"Really!" I worried my clothes would end up just hanging in someone else's closet.

My heart was warmed with the thought of one of my barely used business outfits going to someone who needed it. "I wish her success," I said with mixed emotions. My joy from helping someone out was tinged with grief from letting go of a time that I felt was a highlight in my life.

Sifting through the rest of my belonging revealed some of my silliest obsessions. *Do I really need three large-size tubes of toothpaste from Costco, a case of creamed corn, and these five extra bottles of shampoo that have one more hair washing left in them?*

I was like my dog Zorr (a rescue dog that arrived on our doorstep a year before we departed) that must have had an owner who didn't feed him on time or give him enough food. When I fed Zorr he always left behind a handful of dog food in his bowl, just in case he got hungry before his next meal arrived.

I, too, had this habit, but it was with shampoo, soaps, and lotions. My dependence on lotions and potions had to go; of all my possessions this was the toughest to let go of. I loved that pampered feeling I had when I splurged on buying and using my toiletries.

It took me six months to finish my numerous bottles of shampoo; I was saving for the future. Then I tossed the empty bottles and stopped worrying whether I had enough shampoo.

I never knew I had this unrealistic preoccupation with the future and what I needed when I arrived there. I was so busy working overtime, paying bills, thinking about what to do next, and remembering the past that I missed where I was, the present. I hadn't realized yet that we only have the moment, this time today; we don't know if we will have tomorrow. One of the more painful lessons I would learn on the road.

I was living life so fast I didn't stop to see what my daily activities were doing to me. A glaring sign that my lifestyle wasn't good for me was the amount of over-the-counter medications I took to go to sleep. When I waded through the bottles and packages that cluttered my medicine cabinet I found Nyquil, Benadryl, and various sleep aids. While holding these packages in my hands, I made a promise to myself to slow down. While I was shedding my old life, a new one was being born.

My fancy shampoos were replaced with whatever brand Tim and I could both use, my fancy soap was replaced with cheap hotel soap, you know the kind that makes you skin feel dry. My lotions were all gone and replaced with sunscreen.

I had two pairs of shoes: one for riding the bike and one for walking; six pairs of wool socks; and I traded in my bed sheets for a sleeping bag. I told myself, *that's all I need* as I tried my best to let go. It was a painful disconnect, like losing some kind of solid foundation, my identity. Here is Cindie: she has fifty pairs of shoes, seventy-five shirts, one hundred pairs of socks, and countless bed sheets. She must be a good person (more like a compulsive buyer).

Once the piles began to clear from the house, I felt a sense of relief and freedom from the material objects that were weighing me down. When that change in perception occurred, I was ready to let go of everything.

As the days moved closer to our deadline for leaving (March 30, 2002), I distinctly remember feeling like I was smothered by an octopus and with every load of material possessions I unloaded at the Goodwill or Salvation Army, or into the shed, or into the garbage, I removed one more tentacle that held me down, held me in place like weights chained to my ankles.

Somewhere in those painful moments I changed my view on owning possessions. Somehow I had attached my identity to the clothes I wore, the car I drove, and the bikes I rode. I no longer wanted to be identified that way; instead, I wanted to be defined by my actions, what I did.

The last six months, I was hyper-focused on tying up loose ends. There was so much to do, like finding a property manager I could trust. One property manager wanted to rent the house for less than our mortgage. This didn't sit well with me so I quickly found another. When the new agent said, "Oh, you live in a great neighborhood. I could rent this easily," and "How much is your mortgage? We want to be able to cover that," it was the beginning of a long and trusting relationship.

I still had to close all our bank accounts and find a bank that would allow ATM withdrawals from foreign locations without charging an arm and leg. With each task finished, one more arm of the octopus was removed. We still had to work on packing all our belongings, cleaning the house and yard. We had so much work to do, we barely had time to ride our bikes. I rationalized I could worry about that later and that later was the first week on the bike.

HOW DID YOU FINANCE THE TRIP?

Our monthly expenses, including the mortgage, utilities, and food bill, were a third of my monthly earnings. Tim's take-home pay as a special education teacher was a fifth of my monthly income. I had already paid my student loan and Tim's was paid when we refinanced the house. Our monthly bills were less because our cars were paid for and we didn't have any credit card debt. Reducing our overall expenses and not accumulating debt were crucial to being able to save money.

Before we started putting aside for the trip, I was saving for a new 4-wheel drive truck. I needed a reliable vehicle for work. Rather than have a monthly auto payment, I had planned to pay in cash.

Tim saw my little nest egg growing and suggested we go traveling instead. I wasn't so sure about traveling and compromised with, "Let's continue saving money and talk about this." This was the moment I began reviewing and changing my daily spending habits.

Saving money was a team effort, our motivations may have been different but the outcome was the same. We sat down and assessed our financial health. Awareness was the first weapon in defense of our wallet. We were shocked at how high our monthly bills were and how we were being nickeled and dimed at every turn. Changing our monthly cable, phone, and Internet bill to the lowest possible payment was a hassle but worth the savings. Through our assessment, we realized the vehicles were burning money as fast as they could burn fuel.

My job was in downtown Prescott, a short fifteen-minute drive away; however, I had to drive through four lights and two stop signs. This burned a lot of gas four times a day. Riding my bike to work on days I knew I would be in the office saved money, increased my exercise, and my commute time was almost the same. When I could avoid driving, except for work, I did.

Tim rode his bike to school every day until the principal called him in and said it didn't (that's right, didn't) set a good example. He then showed up in his only vehicle, the RV, and they called the local police. Soon after, he went back to riding his bike to work. We even rode our bikes to most of the club rides.

I packed or ate lunch at home every day. Going out to lunch was reserved for special occasions or meetings. When I ate out, I ordered the cheapest entree on the menu and drank water. This also helped control what I ate.

We had a weekly food allocation and to stay in budget, we bought generic instead of name brands. When I had time, I clipped coupons. I always reviewed the grocery ads and bought the weekly specials. Food didn't go to waste; I usually ate leftovers for lunch. This may sound trivial but all those extra meals add up.

We took stock of what we had in the house and stopped buying food in bulk at Costco nearly a year before we departed. The day we left, we still had cans of food left over. We already had too many tubes of toothpaste, dish soap, floor cleaner, and a big tin of pretzels that were going stale. When I bought something new, I assessed if I needed or wanted it. If I wanted it, I put it back.

In the end, rather than buy a new 4-wheel drive truck, I compromised and got a tune-up and a new paint job instead.

I had some help changing my habits; Tim took the reins of the budget. I didn't mind. I was doing so many other tasks, his frugalness got us from decision, to saving, to out the door in five years.

WHAT WAS YOUR DAILY BUDGET?

At the dreaming stage of the trip I had visions of staying in mid-level hotels and eating out at nice restaurants. That's how I traveled during my vacations so I assumed our bicycle tour would be on a similar budget. Assumptions are usually wrong.

"We can live on thirty dollars a day," Tim announced one afternoon. I thought he was out of his mind and a bit cheap, as well.

"Wait a minute! When I traveled before, I usually had a budget of fifty dollars a day for me alone, not thirty dollars a day for two of us."

"I know honey, but you had a job to come back to then. This time you won't."

"You're right. I won't have a job to come back to and neither will you."

"Don't worry about our trip budget. We will be riding the bikes and that takes out the big expense of transportation."

"Is transportation that expensive?" I asked.

"Oh yes, buses, trains, planes. They're all expensive and we won't be using them much."

"I still don't see how it's that much cheaper," I said.

"Well, we will be staying in the tent for free, too."

"You have a good point. Camping is usually free or at least cheaper," I said. Then asked,

"What is our yearly budget on thirty dollars a day?"

"Let me check my chart. If we travel on thirty dollars a day that's US$10,950 a year."

"Then we should have our savings soon, if we can travel that cheap," I reasoned.

"Exactly," Tim said.

"I don't want to travel that cheap," I interjected.

"We won't. I think we can travel on forty-one dollars a day," Tim replied quickly.

"How much is that a year?"

"Let me check my chart. That's US$14,965 a year."

"Well, we're not quite ready then," I said with a sigh of relief. It wasn't just the budget that wasn't ready yet.

I also wondered what I would do after we returned. Tim didn't give this a second thought. He was bent on leaving and that was where all his energy went.

The transition from living on thirty dollars an hour to thirty dollars a day was an enormous adjustment for me. Letting go of my sense of entitlement to do whatever I desired with my money was difficult.

This changed view of spending money continued on to the road, where it was easier not to buy something because it didn't fit in my pannier. Going out to nice restaurants was especially hard to give up, as well as visiting every tourist site under the sun. How to be content with as little as possible didn't happen overnight nor without confrontation.

WHAT GEAR DID YOU BRING?

I have to say Tim's frugalness went out the window when it came to bicycles and gear; we bought the best quality bicycles for touring. By the time we finished purchasing all our gear, we had depleted a year's worth of travel money. Besides our bicycles, we each bought new bike shoes, helmets, three pairs of bike shorts, two bike jerseys, Gore-Tex and fleece jackets, waterproof booties, helmet covers, sleeping pads, sleeping bags, zip-off travel pants, and six pairs of wool socks. I brought seven pairs of underwear (I had to have a change of underwear for each day of the week, which was an excess when I realized I would be wearing bike shorts every day). I brought them anyway; they were small and didn't take up much room.

We bought all our gear over the Internet and shipped to my office. I usually intercepted the packages before anyone saw them, but I am sure it aroused suspicions in my coworkers and boss. I must admit, I enjoyed shopping for the equipment for our expedition, especially since I was getting rid of all my other belongings.

We carried a mobile kitchen of three titanium pots that fit nicely together (they lasted the entire expedition), a MRS Dragon Fly stove that sounded like a jet engine going off when it was lit (it was temperamental, but easy to clean and put back together), a titanium spork that is a combination of a spoon and fork, a sturdy Buck knife, a Katadyn water filter that filtered out bacteria (proved to be a money and health saver, although Tim had gastro issues three times as often as I did), a large titanium kettle that was Tim's coffee cup (no kidding – could be the source of those gastro issues) and a smaller tin cup for me.

Bathroom accessories included a small shampoo and conditioner, a bottle of SPF 45 sunscreen, toothpaste, toothbrushes and a quick drying towel (yup, I shared a towel with Tim for eight and a half years. How intimate is that?).

Our first tent was large with two doors and could hold all our gear and Tim's large 200-pound-plus frame. Whatever room was left over was for me. The first night in the tent I felt like a pair of shoes stuffed in a shoe box.

WHAT WAS IT LIKE THE DAY YOU LEFT?

Our house was empty, Zorr was in Alaska with my twin sister, and everything I owned was in four panniers (bags) on my bicycle. On our last night in Prescott, Arizona, we slept on the floor of my office.

In the morning, my mind was foggy from lack of sleep and fatigued from overuse. I had made too many decisions over the last week. I pushed my loaded touring bike out the office door and when I jumped on to ride, I couldn't handle the weight and I weaved all over the parking lot. I didn't have far to go (yet), the Prescott Chain Gang bike club was meeting us for breakfast and giving us a sendoff.

I arrived at the restaurant flushed with exertion from the short distance I had pedaled. *Oh boy, keeping my wheels straight is going to take more work than I thought* raced through my mind as I meandered around the parking lot searching for a place to lean my bicycle. The restaurant was filled with familiar faces, emotions were so high the air felt thick, and my wobbly legs barely carried me to the other side of the room. I was overwhelmed by the moral support from the club and especially all the women who were there.

Most of the guys were occupied with how heavy our bikes were and took turns lifting them. They all could easily lift mine, but not Tim's. In addition to the necessities of the trip, he was also carrying a week's worth of canned food. Now it was his turn to carry the burden of our excessive lifestyle.

Breakfast passed in a blur and I couldn't hold back my emotions as we pedaled the short distance from the restaurant to the Court House Square. I had focused so much on the details of leaving that I hadn't mentally prepared myself for the feelings the rose up in me that day. I was ecstatic we had attained our goal of starting our around-the-world bike tour and relieved that I didn't have possessions weighing me down. At the same time, I had a nagging feeling I had left something undone and I knew I would miss my family and friends. My new challenge of handling a wobbly bicycle brought me back to the present, quickly.

More and more people arrived at our starting point and the gathering swelled with people I knew in town. I skimmed the crowd searching for my boss Bill; I had one last task: give back my office key, the last remaining key in my possession. I was also hoping to see him one last time before I left. I knew those chances were slim when he hinted that he didn't like good-byes. My coworker Scott, rather than Bill, came to collect the key. The moment was bittersweet; I was happy to be letting go of the last key I had and was sad that I never really did say good-bye to my mentor. I didn't know it at the time but I never would see him again.

We pedaled out of town with an escort of fifteen other cyclists. I felt insecure those first couple of miles. I worried whether I could pedal the four miles (6.4 kilometers) over the pass leading us away.

As people steadily dropped off to return home, I had a strange sensation that life would be different when I eventually did return. I seriously wondered when that would be. True to what lay ahead for me, my mind was forced back to the present moment to concentrate on getting my loaded touring bike up and over the mountain. It took all my concentration to smooth out my unsteady cycling pace and wobbly steering.

Our first stop was Yarnell, Arizona where we camped for free on BLM (Bureau of Land Management) land for the night. My body hurt everywhere, but my mind was free of a lot of thoughts I didn't need anymore. It was exhilarating and that night I slept the best I had in months.

Our first campsite at Yarnell, Arizona USA.

Riding the back way to Te Anau, near Queenstown, New Zealand.

Chapter 4
What Was It Like Changing Your Lifestyle?

Buying vegetables at a market in Hoi An, Vietnam.

The change from living in a house to carrying everything I owned on a bike was so overwhelming in the beginning, I couldn't pinpoint how that change affected me.

The first week of cycling my body was in revolt. Every muscle ached, I over heated at the drop of a hat, and I sincerely wondered how long it would take my body to stop hurting. Adjusting to my new physical lifestyle took around four weeks. The aches and pains were gone, I felt better, and I was able to ride longer.

During breakfast one morning, I identified what was missing in my life. I didn't have a job that required me to be there five days a week or more. No housecleaning. I no longer owned a mound of clothes that needed washing, folding, and putting away in the right place. I didn't have to open junk mail just to throw it away or shred it because it contained personal information (this one is still my favorite chore I don't have to do). I didn't have to clean the toilet (a very close second, although in my travels I found many toilets that needed cleaning). I didn't fret about paying the bills, because we didn't have any (the bills connected to the house were paid by the tenants). I didn't have to plan meals because we either ate at a restaurant or picked up something easy to cook on our one-burner stove. I didn't worry about my possessions being under lock and key; I didn't have any keys.

Once on the road, my food, shelter, and clothing requirements were reduced to a minimum and this was more liberating than I had expected. I had time to take in my surroundings and I was in awe of what I saw. The complexities of human existence fascinated me and I analyzed my surroundings with a new-found enthusiasm.

While living the western lifestyle, I had expended so much time thinking about work. *What's my new project? What is the problem? What data to collect? What does the data mean?* Suddenly, what had consumed my mind eighty percent of the time was now irrelevant.

My mind revolted like my body had. My thoughts didn't know which way to go. Like most Americans, my job was my identity and being a geologist grounded me. Removing my sense of identity created a void I hadn't expected. This emptiness came out in my dreams; my ego had nothing to cling to. Physically I was away from work, but mentally I was still there. I dreamed about work frequently and not in a good way. A reoccurring theme was forgetting to finish a project. This dream tormented me for nearly six months. It took my mind that long to let go of my working life.

Six months into the trip, my body and mind were in sync with my new lifestyle. Once I let go of the past, I took to being a nomad quite easily. With the daily distractions gone, no need to plan for the future (it was already planned), and the ultra-slow pace of bicycle touring, I had time to think and reflect. I was at the beginning of my spiritual journey, an unintended benefit of shedding a hectic western lifestyle. I had not thought about the spiritual aspect of the bike tour while preparing for our trip. In the end, it was the most important part.

THE CONCEPT OF TIME

My western concept of "time is money" had to change early on. Simply because I no longer made money, and more importantly, the rest of the world had a different concept of time.

On one hand, it was refreshing to be in Mexico where time moved at a much slower pace than in the USA. On the other hand, this slower pace annoyed me. Waiting wasn't something I was used to doing and, at first, I didn't have the tolerance for it. Time is a great teacher (little did I know that there were even more exasperating countries, such as India) and I learned to wait.

When we crossed the border into Mexico, we crossed an invisible time warp as well, and it had a twilight zone feel to it. Stepping out of my country, where we think of time on an hourly basis, and stepping into a country where they think of time on a monthly basis, left me feeling unbalanced. It turns out the rest of the world, except for the developed nations like those in Europe, Scandinavia, UK, Singapore, Japan, Australia, and New Zealand (I wonder which country has the fastest pace) think of time on a monthly basis. Everyone I met in developing countries was paid by the month.

I thought that being paid by the hour and thinking of time on an hourly basis gave us more time. In reality, it made me more impatient. Slowing down and thinking of time on a monthly basis reduced my stress and gave me the sensation (it's all about perception) of having enough time to do what I needed to do. Gradually, I lost that rushed feeling I carried around with me. This unraveling took some time and I was a fidgety mess whenever I had to wait in a line at a market, a bank, or a museum. Learning to calmly wait was crucial to improving my overall health.

My fast-moving western lifestyle had left me wound so tight I couldn't sleep. By loosening up and letting go of time, I improved the quality of my life. I had stumbled upon the reason for my insomnia (besides working too much) – counting the hours in a day, filling them with as much activity as I could, and then perceiving that I didn't have enough time to do it all.

Somehow Tim had already tackled this issue; his motto is only one activity a day. I found this habit to be really maddening until I tried it, then I found the simplicity of dealing with one activity at a time. The time to digest new information and have some empty moments between activities was relaxing. In my hectic life I was running away from these empty moments out of fear of boredom, or fear of not being productive, or fear of what I would find there, myself maybe. I now look for those empty mo-

ments throughout the day to help me relax.
BUYING FOOD AT THE MARKET

Cyclists are constantly hungry. A hungry person thinks about food. When I think of my meandering bike tour around the world, besides the warm and friendly people, I think about the food I ate.

My first encounters with grocery shopping in Mexico still stand out in my mind. The food looked so different from what I was used to buying in supermarkets in the USA. Instead of shopping for a week's worth of groceries at once, I had to buy vegetables at a market that usually happened twice a week.

I couldn't believe how some of the produce looked: oranges had little black spots on them and they weren't even round. I was hesitant to buy an ugly orange or ugly anything. I smelled the orange to make sure it wasn't rotten. It wasn't, so I bought it. When I cut it open and tasted the fruit inside, heaven awaited me; I was greeted with a pungent sweet and juicy flesh. Better than any store-bought orange I had tasted in years.

Throughout the many markets in Mexico, and beyond, I became accustomed to the vast difference in the appearance of vegetables. What was important was how it tasted. Because I didn't have access to a refrigerator, I had to buy vegetables and fruit ripe, ready to eat that day. In addition, while traveling in farming countries, we ate what was in season. This, combined with daily exercise, made me feel much healthier. The food was fresh and tasty, too. I quickly became accustomed to the changes in food supply and quality. Exploring vegetable markets in search of their culinary delights became a highlight in a new town. I am now spoiled by the markets I found around the world.

Years later, on a return trip to the USA, I was overwhelmed by the size and shape of the vegetables I saw in the grocery store. They were bigger, better, and more beautiful than the vegetables I bought in India.

Red onions in India were smaller than a baseball. In the USA they were the size of large softballs (I marveled at how every onion in the pyramid-shaped stack was exactly the same), they looked great. My initial impression of the produce section was sheer delight. Everything was so beautiful I wanted to buy it all.

In comparison, the vegetables in India were smaller and less appealing. In addition, they were garden-fresh for barely a few days. I had to inspect every piece I bought for freshness and bruising. It was worth the effort because the vegetables were full of flavor.

When I got home (in the USA) and cooked those big beautiful red onions, I was disappointed with the taste. There was no flavor. I preferred the small, not-so-beautiful red onions from India. They had more flavor than their counterparts in the USA. I deduced that in the effort to make the onions more eye-appealing, bigger, and more profitable, the farmer (or someone) had somehow removed the taste.

Saturday market in Riobamba, Ecuador.

Part 3 - On the Road

Riding the Cassier highway, Canada.

Chapter 5
What Do You Think About When You're on the Bike?

Cindie talking with Tibetans, Kham region.

When I started cycling around the world, my thoughts were consumed with how my body felt; I had little aches and pains all over. *This seat is too hard. My arms are tired from steering this heavy load. I'm hungry.* I never dreamed I would get that hungry.

Then my thoughts turned to steering a loaded touring bicycle. *Watch out for that hole in the road over there. Don't look past the shoulder of the road, I'll go there. That car came way too close for my comfort.*

First lesson on bike handling skills, the bike goes where I look. If I don't want to go "there" (like over the edge of a cliff), don't look, "there". Second lesson, drivers are not alert when they are talking or texting on the phone. Never assume they see you.

Slowly, as all the aches and pains disappeared, and I grew more comfortable with my bike handling skills, my mind began to wander and it usually landed where I was or what I was experiencing at that moment.

To my surprise, my thoughts were consumed by three topics: politics, economics, and religion. All subjects I had thought were quite boring before I left on our bike tour. Observing these influences – on people's livelihood, standard of living, and happiness – changed my focus.

In Mexico, I saw economic change. It was 2002 and Mexican men were migrating north to the USA to fill job vacancies. That combined with an increased demand for labor at maquiladoras (factories) in Mexico due to NAFTA (North America Free Trade Agreement) left positions open in other parts of Mexico. A financial and labor shift was under way.

In Guatemala, I witnessed widespread poverty at a level I hadn't seen before. Experiencing this shifted my perception of my own life.

In Southeast Asia, I was heart stricken with the atrocities of war, from the Killing Fields in Cambodia, to the Chu Chi tunnels in Vietnam, and the remnants of an old American military base in Laos. I sympathized with the victims of war and wondered how the human race continued to inflict cruel and senseless acts of violence on others.

In the USA, in 2008, I wondered how my country had gotten into such a financial mess, was overwhelmed by the material excess I saw, disappointed by the number of homeless people, and shocked by the number of Vietnam War vets who were living in our state and national parks on the west coast. *Don't we have a way to take care of them?*

In the Tibetan area of the Himalayas, I marveled at how life and religion are so closely tied. My interest in Tibetan Buddhism began in 2005, but I didn't have time to learn more until I settled down in McLeod Ganj, India, home of the Dalai Lama and a large Buddhist population.

In the Hmong areas of Laos I contemplated what it would be like to be oppressed by a government I fought against and lost.

MEXICO

I recall many experiences in Mexico, our first country to cycle through, with emotion. During the transition from my previous life to a nomadic one, I had no idea what to expect from our travels. People's reactions toward me on the bike were new; I was repeatedly surprised by the kindness and generosity extended to me. Relaxing, my thoughts moved to the human condition. It was a natural tendency to compare my lifestyle in the

USA with what I saw around me. What I realized early on was that I had a higher standard of living than most people.

Traveling southward on our bikes we continuously met men going north to work.

In my discussions with English-speaking natives, most people from Mexico would prefer to stay close to their families at home. Low wages in Mexico and higher wages in neighboring USA for the same work, motivated mostly men to travel north. I wondered what the economic and social impacts were on those left behind.

Some of the changes were easy to see. When the men left Mexico they created a vacuum of labor; women quickly moved into those positions. Women were running Internet cafés, restaurants, and travel agencies. I was witnessing a revolution. Women were changing roles and were happy to give up having twenty kids – literally – and work outside the home.

In 2003, two percent of Mexico's gross domestic product (GDP), an indicator of the overall standard of living of a country, was money coming from relatives living in the USA[1].

GUATEMALA

Getting off the pity pot

I thought I had seen poverty in Mexico. I hadn't. The level of existence in Guatemala was even more basic. Most homes had very few store-bought items, and everything, including their home and clothes, were handmade. It was apparent, from the first day we crossed the border from Mexico into La Mesilla, Guatemala, that the poverty level was higher in Guatemala than Mexico. It reminded me of the stark contrast at the border between the USA and Mexico, however, this was one rung lower.

On our way out of town, I saw people rummaging through a smelly trash pile. *What are these people doing in a trash pile?* Then it struck me. They were searching for food or something to sell. Standing not too far from me near the edge of the road was a young girl, maybe eight or nine. My heart ached for this child with unruly hair and torn T-shirt who stared as I pedaled by. I was quite unnerved by the scene.

Early in my career, I investigated landfills for environmental permitting purposes so I knew how toxic they could be. It really disturbed me that the best these people could do was comb through other people's garbage. Trash in Guatemala was far different (probably more toxic) from trash in the USA. It was survival I had not seen before; human beings reduced to an animal's existence.

For the next four days we steadily rode uphill through a canyon past clusters of homes lining the road. The concrete houses had discarded building materials tacked on here and there, and the porches were constructed from homemade adobe bricks.

The friendly women in homemade clothing, who waved to us, seemed content to weave garments in the morning sun. A simple loom, a piece of wood with yarn tied to it, hung from the wall held taut by a strap around the weaver. A young woman knelt on the porch while she threaded colored yarn ranging from mustard yellow to eggplant purple through the loom. By the appearance of their clothing, I assumed when the piece she was working on was finished, it probably went to a family member to wear.

We also passed a group of men making adobe bricks by hand. Whole families walked by carrying firewood on their backs, while we sat and enjoyed our lunch on the side of the road. Everyone had a burden, from grandpa to grandson. Women carried everything on their heads from vases full of water to vegetables. I had never seen this vast a number of people struggling so hard to eat and stay alive.

Four days later we arrived in the town of Huehuetenango, population of around 80,000. In the main plaza we sat and took a break before venturing around town to find a room. Stretched along one side of the square stood an old colonial building with high arches, the peeling yellow paint made it look shabby. Scattered throughout town were abandoned buildings and falling down walls.

This area of Guatemala saw heavy fighting during the civil war that raged from 1960 to 1996. The battle was between the Mayans and descendants of the first Spanish and European landowners with the landowners eventually winning. The scars of war were visible in this predominately indigenous town that was coming back to life. Despair, sadness, and struggle were visible in the way people walked down the street. The feel of town frightened me because the low economic existence was tinged with a heavy sense of hopelessness.

I was out of my comfort zone in Huehuetenango; most people there existed below poverty level, in the city and the surrounding countryside.

Being an optimistic American from a well-off country, hopelessness wasn't something I had often personally experienced. It was then I realized that I was a member of a privileged group of people who had hope, optimism, and enough material belongings to survive. The biggest myth in my life evaporated like a mirage and the evaporation process was painful. That myth being, I grew up poor and more importantly the self-pity I harbored because of that experience. More details on this later (Lessons From the Road, Chapter 15).

CAMBODIA

Mid-December 2004 we crossed the border from Aranyaprathet, Thailand into Cambodia. I wasn't looking forward to meeting the generation who had survived the atrocities of Pol Pot and the Khmer Rouge, who killed a quarter (the educated portion) of the population (approximately two million) between 1975 and 1979. Five years prior to the communist takeover, Cambodia struggled through a civil war marred by foreign intervention and heavy bombing. As a result, Cambodia still has a large number of unexploded ordinances (bombs) scattered around the country.

My expectation of meeting sad and miserable people never materialized. Instead, greeting me were crowds of children who were delighted to meet me, practice English, and at one point tried to get me to eat "snake" not "steak." My mind kept insisting they said "steak," probably wishful thinking. I confirmed the locals did indeed eat "snake," a delicacy I wasn't ready to try.

As we cycled toward Siem Reap, I saw a number of people with missing legs. I wondered if they had wandered into the wrong place. Thinking about life without legs to pedal a bicycle or walk, made me cringe and caused my legs to twitch. I reached down and touched my thigh, happy to have my legs and my health all the more.

When we finally arrived in Siem Reap, we blended back into the tourist scene, but I still couldn't get the local people off my mind. All along the road we met the remaining members of a generation who had experienced genocide. I could see it on their faces. One woman must have suffered immensely because her face was frozen in shock; she looked as though she had witnessed the execution of her entire family. I could see, as well as feel, her pain and suffering.

She remains in my mind to this day, reminding me that people can be cruel beyond my imagination. I wonder whether she is really surviving or just suffering through an unbearable human existence.

USA – THE IMPACT OF ECONOMICS

September 2008 we returned, six and a half years after starting our expedition, to the lower forty-eight through Port Angeles, Washington. It wasn't long before the stock market crashed and housing prices dropped. What I witnessed as I traveled through my own country was heartbreaking. Home after home was for sale. Garage sales with everything people owned sat on driveways. This wasn't like my garage sale when I left on my around-the-world trip. This was to sell everything to pay the bills; a very different mindset.

Searching for an answer, I reflected on what seemed to be different in the short time I was gone, concluding material excess appeared to be over the top. I heard people were using their homes like ATMs, refinancing and then buying cars, other homes, and new phones. In Alaska and down the West Coast, three or four cars, a quad, a riding lawn mower, and a motorcycle adorned many homes. All I could think about was the amount of gasoline that must be consumed to power all these machines.

Recovery from this economic disaster was going to take time. These events impacted my life as well; there were no jobs for a geologist who had taken over six years off to go on a bike tour. Along with many fellow Americans, I had to adjust to the changing economic environment.

POLITICAL OPPRESSION

Tibetans – The Impact of Religion

September 2005, I met my first Tibetan when Tim and I stopped for lunch at a small café in the foothills of the Himalayas. Before the waiter took our order, he pulled out a photo of the Dalai Lama from around his neck and showed it to us. I responded with, "The Dalai Lama," and his face lit up. He quickly returned his precious photo under his shirt for safekeeping. I knew he could go to jail for possessing that photo. Many Tibetans have, but that danger wasn't apparent at that moment.

He served us a bowl of noodles and a Pepsi each. When we paid the bill he didn't charge for the Pepsis and gestured they were a gift from him.

He also expressed his concern for our safety on the bikes with hand signals demonstrating a car pushing us off the road. Then he said, "Cold," in English and pointed up into the mountains. At the same time, he gave himself a bear hug, shook up and down, and then had a huge belly laugh. He was right, it was cold, but I didn't find it quite as funny.

I already knew the Chinese had invaded Tibet in 1950 and the Dalai Lama had fled to India in 1959. What I didn't know was what was happening in Tibet while the Dalai Lama continues to be in exile.

Considering what it would be like to be occupied by another, like the Hmong (see below) and the Tibetans, left me feeling empty. In one generation, the Chinese government had systematically destroyed Tibetan Buddhist temples and monasteries that were hundreds of years old, removed the Tibetan language from schools, poisoned the tenth Panchen Lama, the highest spiritual leader remaining in Tibet, and kidnapped his reincarnate and his family. The Tibetan culture was being dismantled at an alarming rate as well; traditional dress, dance, poetry, and writing were being wiped out one artist at a time.

My first introduction to Tibetan Buddhism in China was in Inner Mongolia where I visited a 250-year-old monastery that once housed 1,200 monks, tulkus (recognized reincarnates) and lamas (teachers) who studied mathematics, the Tibetan calendar and astronomy, Buddhist philosophy, and Tibetan medicine and history.

The day I visited the monastery it was empty. I saw maybe ten monks that day and it was obvious the temples and dormitories were not in use. What I didn't realize then was the same was happening in Tibet, over 1,200 miles (1,931 kilometers) away. The monasteries were being closed and the monks sent home. It wasn't just the Tibetans who were under siege from the Chinese. Throughout history, Han Chinese had conquered and dismantled minority cultures. The Hmong culture, language, and traditions had already been destroyed by them centuries earlier.

Hmong - Laos

December 2005 we entered Laos. Most of the people living in the northern hill country are Hmong. The same minority group who live in the mountainous regions of Vietnam, Thailand and China. In the early 1700s, political persecution and economic repression initiated their exodus from China into surrounding countries.

During the Vietnam War, the Hmong were recruited by the CIA (Central Intelligence Agency)[2] to fight against communism in Laos and that communist face was the Pathet Lao, an equivalent to the Viet Cong. When the Vietnam War ended, America withdrew from Vietnam and Laos, as well. Except for a few high-level commanders who were evacuated by the CIA, most of the recruited Hmong fighters were left behind.

The Hmong people were either pushed up into the hilly areas of Laos or fled into the neighboring country of Thailand. The people who escaped to Thailand remained refugees for nearly thirty-five years. Then, on December 28, 2009, Thai soldiers rounded up the remaining Hmong refugees and sent them back to Laos. Six years earlier, Thai authorities helped relocate 14,000 Hmong to the USA. How confusing that must have been to the helpless people in those refugee camps.

Where are they now? From what I have seen in other communist countries, they were likely placed in re-education camps or have been executed. This is the ugly side of human interaction, sadly Southeast Asia had more than its share of violent clashes.

While traveling through western China, northern Laos and eastern Thailand, I contemplated what it would be like to be a refugee and I couldn't come close to understanding what that felt like. I will never know the anguish of losing my home, language, or culture.

In comparison to the Tibetans and Hmong, I have many liberties including religious freedom; I can become a Buddhist. Even if my Christian family doesn't agree, I can still change. I am free to dress the way I want, listen to the music I like, and read the New York Times that prints what they choose due to our Second Amendment, freedom of speech. The more I travel the more I am grateful for the freedoms extended to me because I grew up in a democracy.

Chapter 6
How Did People React To You?

Cindie and Andy riding through a small village in northern Laos.

How people reacted to us depended on where we were, how we were dressed, and where they were from. Tourist zones were different than rural areas. We got a different reaction when we were in bike clothes than in street clothes. On more than one occasion, people didn't recognize us away from the bikes. Finally, where people were from played a role in their reaction to us. In general, people from developing countries wanted to meet us while people from developed countries saw us as other tourists.

Traveling in rural areas of China, Mexico, and Bolivia was similar; we were greeted with enthusiasm, especially from children, and most farmers stopped working in the field to wave as we pedaled by.

Tourist areas like Cusco, Peru and Agra, India were full of touts (sellers) looking to make money off visitors. We were just tourists. In these areas, fending off touts was like swatting at a cloud of mosquitos; when I brushed one aside another came in for the kill. I always tried to be polite when I declined whatever they were selling, which worked well in keeping situations from getting irritating.

Other western tourists were a quirky bunch; some ignored us, pretending they were the only ones there (this happened in remote areas). Other westerners listened in on our conversations at restaurants, but never talked to us (practicing their English maybe). While others asked lots of questions about traveling by bicycle.

Children were the same everywhere, greeting us with enthusiasm. In some places, we drew crowds of curious children who were not afraid to meet the newcomers to town. Most wanted to wear our helmets, some wanted to ride our bikes, and all wanted to ring our bells. A bike is not frightening to a child; perhaps riding it just looks like fun.

On a few occasions, adults wanted to ride my bike and after the first one crashed and fell on the ground, I was more choosy about who got to do a test ride.

LATIN AMERICA

After a couple of months in Mexico, a local man who had just stepped out of a restaurant and saw me on the sidewalk asked, "Where are you from?"

"North America," I responded.

"Are you poor?" he asked in a sincere manner.

"No. Why do you ask?"

"Because you are riding a bicycle, not the bus," he replied then added, "All foreigners ride the bus."

I had to chuckle at the thought of people thinking I was poor. I really didn't mind, but it was funny they thought I should be riding the bus. "I like to ride my bicycle, not the bus," I claimed.

"Good. Enjoy Mexico," is all he said, while he scratched his forehead still confused about why I wouldn't travel the easy way.

Overwhelmingly (and at times the most annoying) the first question most people in Latin America asked was, "How many children do you have?"

The first time someone asked we lied and told them our children were in college. One white lie led to another and another. Before we knew it, our lack of children had turned into a mythical daughter and son of college age. This didn't sit well with either of us; I felt awful lying to strangers. And for what reason? To fit into their cultural norm. This wasn't a pleasant experience for me nor Tim.

We continued to modify our response. I once tried, "We are trying, but we are having no luck." Before I knew it I was dragged into the kitchen by the woman of the house, Maria, and her friend, Gloria. Maria spoke Spanish so fast I understood just a couple of words. While she made me a cup of tea, she chattered as if I comprehended every word.

All I could decipher from her rapid Spanish was that she concluded I was the one who couldn't have children. When Maria finished preparing her concoction, she handed me a cup of bitter tea I wanted to spit out. I nurtured that tea for over a half hour before I finally finished it.

Then one day Tim came up with a brilliant response that went something like this, "Maybe, if we are lucky, we will have a child in nine months." That was it. That was the answer. Everyone laughed, they gave us privacy, if we were staying with them, and, most of all, we weren't spinning a web of lies.

LAOS

Laos has many small villages of five or six homes clustered, straddling the side of the roads. The homes have a temporary feel to them because they don't have running water or electricity. Each is made of a thatched roof and walls and is raised above the ground on stilts. This keeps the home cool during the hot dry season (Laos has a tropical monsoon climate), from getting flooded during the rainy season, and vermin, such as snakes, scorpions, and wandering boars, out. The last reason would be the most important to me, as the thought of snakes slithering between thatched-filled mattresses comes to mind.

The people were a joy to meet, especially the children. It soon became obvious that it was a game for the kids in the villages to run to the side of the road and yell, "sabadee," "hello" in Lao, as we slowly pedaled past. Some of these kids barely had any clothes on, or none at all. At other times, five or six little ones would sing to us as we wandered through their tiny village. I couldn't help but enjoy all the attention. At the end of the day, my heart was warmed and my arms were sore from waving to every child.

WESTERNERS

While traveling in developed countries such as Australia, New Zealand, Canada, and the USA, we usually got one of two reactions: excitement or disbelief. A few were interested in our trip, some thought "good on ya" or "go for it" in American slang, some thought we were crazy – why would you want to do that? This, to me, was the most understandable reaction. And finally, "you are just plain stupid". Hmm. It is interesting the things you learn when you understand the language.

Kindness of Strangers

I tried to count the number of people who offered us a place to stay, a beer, a ride, food, (we must have always looked hungry as people were always feeding us) souvenirs, or a tour of the local sites during our travels, but it is far too many to tally.

Generosity and kindness warmed my heart frequently. This reoccurring response from strangers strengthened my belief that people are good and has inspired me to behave the same way toward other people. However, it will take me a lifetime to repay all the hospitality I have received on the road. A few encounters come to mind when I think of the kindness of strangers.

Hobart, Tasmania

Two days before arriving in Hobart, Tasmania, we called our first WarmShowers.com host (a free worldwide hospitality exchange for touring cyclists). Unfortunately, the cyclist in the family wasn't home but his wife was; we stayed for two days. She cooked us a typical Australian meal of meat on the barbie (barbecue) and showed us tourist sites such as the botanical garden in Hobart.

Sydney, Australia

Carol and Mark, in Sydney, had been following my online journal for quite some time, so, when we were near their home, they invited us to stay a few days. We quickly settled into their upscale apartment where, for entertainment, rather than watching TV we had a floor-to-ceiling library of books and CDs to browse. It was a real pleasure going through their stacks of books and picking something to read.

Ruatoria, New Zealand

When we reached Ruatoria, New Zealand, we were burnt out from tackling the steepest hills on the East Cape. Arriving on Boxing Day (the day after Christmas) was a problem. Almost everything was closed and we couldn't find a place to camp in town. We went with our standard plan of picking up water and riding until we found a place to camp somewhere outside of town. I went inside a store and bought two of New Zealand's delicious ice cream cones. When I returned to the bikes, Tim was talking to

Harold, the owner of the shop next door. Harold was happy to give us water and when he found out we needed a place to camp he said, "Come with me. You can camp in my back yard." To top it off, he let us take a shower at his shop – not an ordinary shower, but a rainwater shower. Rainwater is softer than surface or groundwater and easily removed the buildup of sunscreen on my body.

Cyclists

Laos

The first climb out of Luang Prabang, Laos was quick and at the top of the hill we took a break. There we met an American cyclist who had been on the road for over three years. The years on the road showed on him like a neon sign in Las Vegas. His clothes were torn and dirty and I got the impression he had been sleeping under a bush all night. His bike was broken, too; it had a crack on the top bar from an accident in Thailand. He had had someone weld the steel tube back together, but the thick uneven weld didn't look like it would hold much longer. Even his speech was choppy and unfocused, probably because he hadn't spoken English in awhile. I thought it might be time for him to get off the road.

The encounter frightened me because he didn't seem to know he was burnt out. I honestly didn't want to become that run down. I prayed I would know when it was time to stop.

Two days later, we met Andy at a guesthouse at the top of a long exhausting climb. He wandered into town and to our dinner table just before dark. He was cycling from England to Singapore where he had a job waiting for him. We cycled together for a few days in Laos, played leap frog all the way to Bangkok, Thailand. We met Andy again in Singapore, where he showed us the finest places to dine and other odd tourist sites in town.

Australia

After Singapore, we toured Australia where nearly every cyclist we met online or in town invited us to stay in their home. The Melbourne Bike Touring Club introduced us to the many rides in their area and we explored the features of Melbourne with them via the well-planned bike lanes and paths.

USA

On the west coast of the USA, we came across large groups of touring cyclists. My favorite group was the surfers who towed their boards down the coast in search of the ultimate wave. Cooking was also their passion. The surfer/touring cyclists took turns preparing gourmet meals over a campfire. It was a joy to visit their campfire/kitchen in the evening.

Our hiker/biker campsite and Honeyman State Park, Oregon, USA.

Chapter 7
Were You Ever Scared?

Cindie riding into a tunnel near Mendoza, Argentina.

Sometimes being scared is a personal decision, while other times there is truly something to be frightened by, then there are times when your fright is comical, like a grown up who is frightened by a mouse (this wasn't Tim, it was me and the mouse was a rat).

The biggest fear I had to conquer on the road was of the unknown. Once I released myself from that, my other fears reoccurred so many times I had to let go of them too. So if you're wondering if I am more fearless now, I would say yes. It was a different story at the beginning though.

CROSSING THE BORDER INTO MEXICO

We were on our way to Douglas, Arizona (on the border with Mexico), we stopped for a lunch break under a tree by the side of the road. As we ate our tortillas and avocado, a large metallic blue pickup truck slowed down and pulled over onto the sandy shoulder. A tall man in a cowboy hat and boots stepped out of his truck and strolled over to see what we were doing.

"Afternoon folks. It's hot today. Would you like a cold pop?" he asked.

"Sure," We echoed in unison. I surveyed his pickup with a quad in the back and blurted out, "What's the quad for?" before I could stop myself.

"Well, we have trouble with illegals in these parts. If I hear some are in the area, I'll chase them down, pin them down, and then call ICE."

"Do what? Call who?" I stuttered.

"ICE. Immigration and Customs Enforcement," he replied.

"You mean you chase them down like animals?" I had visions of how terrifying that would be.

"Well, Ma'am, yes. They cause a lot of trouble on my ranch. Almost weekly, I have to repair a cut line to a water tank for my cattle because some illegal is thirsty and cuts the line to get a drink. When they do that they empty the tank and I have no water for my cattle."

"I do see the problem. Isn't there a better way to fix it, like giving people work visas?" I asked.

"I don't know about that Ma'am. All I know is they keep cutting my water lines."

He opened my eyes to the complexity of the situation at the border. Still I couldn't help but think chasing people down on a quad was inhumane.

Years later, I heard about Robert Krentz, (to this day I wonder if he was the same man) who was gunned down in March 2010 while checking water lines on his property. His murder was never solved, but federal agencies suspected a smuggler was responsible[3].

The time had come to leave the comforts of our home country and venture into the unknown. From now on we would be foreigners in other countries.

May 13, 2002, we pedaled across the border from Douglas, Arizona to Agua Prietà (meaning brown water – how fitting) Mexico.

We quickly passed through immigration and were on the other side, in Mexico. From there on out we were like salmon swimming upstream. While we set our sights for places south, it appeared the rest of the world was going north. We were seeking a new way of life and so were they; it was odd we were looking for a better life in each other's back yard. *What did I have that they didn't?* The sheer difference in numbers going the other way told me I had a better life in America. I must have been crazy for riding by bicycle in the wrong direction, but there was no turning back.

My adrenaline rush at the border must have increased my sense of smell. I was almost knocked off my bicycle by the putrid decaying garbage smell of town (an all too common odor in many parts of the world). It oozed through my nose and down my throat; I could taste it. This sent my stomach into wild turns and tears ran down my cheeks.

I gripped my handlebars a little too hard while thoughts of turning around danced in my head. Lyle, one of my co-workers sang his warning in my ear, "You're going to get killed the moment you cross the border." Well, I was in that moment. I looked around at the filthy streets and half-built cars and knew he was right. I had descended into a nightmare (I would later discover most border towns look this way). I secretly hoped life would not end there.

Getting out of town was painfully slow, but once we did the traffic quieted down, the air smelled fresh again, and I could hear myself think. Occasionally, a large double trailer would ramble by and, to my disappointment, the road paralleled the border rather than away from it, as I expected.

That night we camped away from the road, but still very close to the USA/Mexico border. As we scouted around for a place to camp, we discovered stacks of belongings scattered throughout the desert. The pile of children's clothes and toys was the most disturbing to me. I couldn't imagine the desperation it took to attempt a desert crossing into Arizona. I wondered whether the people who had abandoned their belongings had made it through the inhospitable desert in the middle of May.

My fears, of not knowing the language or getting lost or robbed, were nothing in comparison. I had a home I could return to, enough food to eat, and the skills to take care of myself. These people had no safety net.

TUNNELS

Guanajuato, Mexico

We had been traveling in Mexico for almost two months when we made a short detour to Guanajuato, Mexico where we studied Spanish for a few weeks, danced salsa through the night, and conquered the underground tunnels of town by day.

Guanajuato is an old silver mining town located in a bowl-shaped valley in central Mexico. As is common with many mining towns, the city lies above the mining operation.

For centuries, floods plagued the city during the rainy season, and in the 1960s large ditches and tunnels were built through the mountain to divert the floodwaters to the outside world. Those passages are used for transportation in and out of the city during the dry season.

One afternoon after class, we explored the city by bicycle and exited town through one of its many tunnels. Going through the down-gradient tunnels was quick and easy on the way out. On our return, however, the grade was uphill and slow-going on the bicycle. To my dismay, the first tunnel was too long to see to the other side. The light of day disappeared into the throat of the mountain. I stood at the tunnel entrance, my heart pounding in my ears, the hairs on my arms stood up, and a shiver traveled down my spine. I thought, *Nope, I am not riding. I can walk this.*

Tim tried to convince me to ride behind him but I stubbornly refused.

"I can walk," I said. I assumed it would be safer (at least my feet would be on the ground) than riding.

As I pushed my bicycle into the tunnel, the last image I saw before the light disappeared altogether was a dead puppy on the side of the road. In a flash, I changed my mind. While screaming like a crazy woman, I hopped on my bicycle and pedaled deep into the darkness of the tunnel until my lungs were ready to explode. The tunnel was longer than my lungs could handle, my body slowed from the lack of oxygen, but my mind urged me on. I surged out the other side and found Tim waiting in the sunshine on the side of the road.

I pedaled over to him, dropped my bike on the ground with a thud, bent over in a crouched position, and began to hyperventilate. I thought I was going to pass out. After patiently waiting for me to get over my panic attack, Tim said, "Ah, Cindie. You better get ahold of yourself. We are not done with the tunnels yet."

"What?" I yelled, while trying to catch my breath.

"We are standing in the middle of two tunnels. At least that's what I think. It could be more. To get back to Guanajuato we need to ride through at least one more tunnel."

"No!" I grumbled, "This isn't fair." My energy was already depleted from the adrenaline rush in the first tunnel. My muscles were fatigued and my confidence shot. Somehow, I had to talk myself into moving on. Tim insisted I eat something and that made me feel better.

"Breathe. Breathe," I repeated over and over until I was ready to set off.

Tim turned his taillight on, took the lead, and said, "I will ride slow enough for you to stay with me. Just concentrate on the taillight. You will be OK."

With that, we shoved off into the dark tunnel and when the final ray of light disappeared it felt like something had tightened around my heart. My fear had a grip on me. I concentrated on the taillight the best I could. Cars whizzed past us so fast. I knew if I made one small mistake and turned into their path I would end up like the puppy in the first tunnel. We burst out the other side quicker than I anticipated. "I need a break," was all I could say.

I had made it through the second tunnel alive, unlike the puppy. We took a break and then pedaled slowly back to our room. Mentally and physically exhausted, I stayed in our hotel room the rest of the day.

While in my self-induced seclusion, I mused why I wasted so much energy on fear. It really bothered me that I had lost control so easily, and, assessing the situation, I realized I had created the problem myself. *Why?* I churned this thought for days. The image of the dead puppy kept reappearing, as if trying to tell me something, and it finally did.

It became clear to me early one morning; riding into a dark tunnel is what I imagine death to be like. When life ends, we enter darkness, and we don't know what happens next. I resolved it is really death that I am afraid of, and the darkness of the tunnel is a trigger for that fear.

I would undergo a similar 'death' many more times, thirty-six times in one day in Peru. By the last one I had come to terms with my disorientation in the darkness of tunnels.

Farther south in Chile, I again had to pedal as hard as I could, uphill through a tunnel, but at an elevation of 10,000 feet (3,049 meters). Fear gripped me once more, but this time I felt a tinge of familiarity as I pedaled into the depths of the mountain. I had made it through so many others. I knew I would make it through this one; familiarity made the experience so much easier.

Every continent has tunnels. When we reached western China, in the fall of 2005, we encountered another tunnel marathon. These ranged from one to four miles (two to six kilometers) in length. The Chinese have trumped the rest of the world with building engineering marvels and nightmares at the same time.

Again, I had to confront my fear of death; only I was armed with some ammunition this time, knowledge. I had ridden through so many tunnels I knew I would come out the other side. Still, right before entering the tunnel I cleared my mind and chanted, *I can do this, I can do this.* On the other side I was relieved to not have succumbed to the darkness. I know that some day I will face death but if I face it with a clear and calm mind, it will be better than entering into the darkness in a panic.

DOGS

Anyone who rides a bicycle has been chased by a dog. If you haven't yet, you will. I think of it as the dark side of cycling. There's something about riding into a dog's territory, and riding out again that drives them crazy. As with most of my fears, this one started in childhood. On the way home from school one day, when I was nine years old, I spotted a large German shepherd, or he spotted me. Either way, I ran. The dog quickly pursued, nipping at my heels. Running for the trees ahead of me, somehow I got stuck circling a large tree in a cement planter. Like that was going to protect me from the big guy. It didn't. He bit my lower left leg, leaving a tiny puncture wound from one of his fang teeth.

Periodically, through my adult years, I would gaze down at my scar and be reminded of that episode; I remembered nearly fainting in fear. Looking back now, I roar with laughter at myself for running in circles around a tree only to be bitten by the dog anyway.

Running away from fear is like running away from the German shepherd of my youth. My fears will always follow me, no matter what country I am in, until I stop and face them. During my travels by bicycle, I had to stop and face my fear of dogs over and over again.

On our bicycle tour, I can remember being chased by dogs at least once in every country. The nastiest, or so I thought at the time, were the sheep dogs we encountered high in the Andes from Ecuador to Argentina.

Being a stubborn person, (who holds on to her phobias as if they are treasures) I couldn't let go of my fear of dogs. But the universe had other plans for me: repeat and repeat until I got it. Slowly that stubborn person, me, began to understand the behaviors of dogs.

Dogs have a pack mentality. One dog alone is different from two or more dogs; they move with the alpha dog. If Tim or I could confront it, the others would stay back to watch what would happen. When we could win the battle with the alpha dog, which Tim usually did, the other dogs dropped off.

Dogs are territorial. If I wanted to get away from them, I had to get out of their territory. Unfortunately, dogs don't post any signs identifying where their neighborhood ends. I needed to find the imaginary line, defined by them, and get beyond it as fast as I could.

These lessons came in handy while living in India where stray dogs are in abundance. Most will pick an area of town to live in (their territory), sleep all day, and bark all night. The annoying all-night barking is part of living in India. I believe the poor things are either hungry or lonely or sending out the alarm an intruder is in the area.

My fear of dogs has come full circle. I began my travels with a healthy fear of dogs. OK, maybe a little unhealthy. Through time and numerous encounters with them, I became familiar with their behaviors and realized that most of the time I can get away from them. Territory is a big issue with dogs, so the faster I left the better.

GUNS
Laos

It was December 2005 and we had just arrived in Laos, our third communist country. We had spent the previous year in China and Vietnam where the chance of seeing a gun was close to nil. Traffic on the road was light with just one car or truck passing us once every hour or two. The vegetation was thick, semitropical jungle, beautiful to see yet strangely out of balance because of the unnerving silence; not a rustle in the bushes nor a chirp from the branches.

I was settled into a nice riding pace for the uphill grid, humming to a Neil Young tune coming from Tim's handlebar bag. We rounded a corner and saw two men wearing army fatigues and black boots with guns strapped to their backs. In their hands were sling shots (I thought only little boys hunted with slingshots – I was mistaken). The guns were pointing toward the ground, but that didn't make them any less ominous. I've watched enough movies to know that the guns were AK-47s.

My body reacted quicker to the sight of the guns than my mind. Sweat drenched my hands and most of my body, I felt nauseous, and then my spiked adrenaline thrust me into action. I stomped on my pedals as if going uphill harder would make the situation go away. It didn't. Laos suddenly didn't feel safe for riding anymore. *Are these men friends or foes?* echoed in my head.

"Look at those guns. I think we should get on a bus," I announced to Tim.

"Hang on there Cindie. Just relax," he responded.

I knew Laos had its share of dangers, like unexploded ordinances, better known as bombs, left over from the war (the Vietnam War spilled over into Laos, although I don't remember learning that in school) so camping or even stepping off the pavement wasn't recommended. I hadn't considered the possibility of a soldier walking around with an AK-47.

My instinct was to flee, but Tim wasn't going anywhere, so I was forced to slow down. Instead, I bit my lower lip and pushed on in hopes that Laos was more concerned with its image with the outside world than it was in harassing a couple of foreign cyclists.

We passed the gun-toting men without incident, except for my pounding heart, that is. Farther down the road, we saw men carrying AK-47s getting on a bus. I wouldn't have wanted to be on that bus.

GETTING ARRESTED IN CHINA

Not long after entering China in April 2005, we had the scariest experience of the entire trip. That episode changed my view of China, which I am thankful for, because if it hadn't happened I don't think I would have believed the crazy, suspicious, conspiracy-theory type behavior the Chinese government displayed while we were in China.

In contrast, the Chinese people were kind, gentle, helpful, funny, trusting, great cooks, had a different view of hygiene than I had, and accepted spitting in restaurants and public places like a westerner would accept smoking.

I can't say I wasn't warned by a straight-talking Brit I met on a train in Bolivia. "The Chinese people are lovely if you can get past the spitting," she said. She was right. What she should have added was, it isn't what is left on the floor, it is the sound of it getting there that is unnerving. A cultural clash I had a hard time adjusting to the entire time I was in China.

Thirteen days after our arrival in China, our eyes were opened to a system we had no idea existed, a system the Chinese government wanted to keep from the outside world.

It started innocently enough with a photo.

"Take a picture of the farmers," I said to Tim, not realizing it would lead to seeing our first gun in Asia, removal of our camera and passports, arrest, detention and interrogation, intimidation, embarrassment during a search of our belongings, pressure to sign a confession, return of camera and passports, release, and worst of all, being followed for three days.

In the end, we still had the photos, and a week later, when we finally gathered up the nerve to examine our memory stick, the pictures were still there. On a second review, the farmers were dressed like prisoners. Maybe they appeared to be like prisoners because the second time I saw the photo I was expecting to see prisoners. A detailed account of our arrest in China can be found in my book, *Finding Compassion in China: A Bicycle Journey into the Countryside.*

The Chinese prisoners I thought were farmers.

A tower on the Great Wall of China.

Chapter 8
What Was It Like Getting Visas and Crossing Borders?

Crossing the border from Thailand to Cambodia.

Every country has different visa requirements, length of stays, and costs. It also depends on nationality: visa requirements for Americans are different than Canadians.

Border crossings were the most stressful days of the trip. Most of the time, the language, money, and standard of living changed once we crossed an imaginary line at a gate, usually guarded by men with guns.
VISAS

In 2002 and 2003, Latin America, including Argentina, Bolivia, Chile, Costa Rica, Ecuador, Guatemala, Honduras, Mexico, Panama, and Peru didn't have visa requirements for Americans visiting as tourists. All allowed a ninety-day stay at the border at no cost, except for Mexico that allowed 180 days at a cost of twenty US dollars each. We paid one US dollar and thirty cents each to leave Guatemala; five US dollars each to get our bikes out of Honduras; four US dollars for a tourist card and three US dollars entrance fee each for Nicaragua. We never knew when a random fee charged by some levy dispensing official would occur.

Asia was a different story altogether where every country charged for a visa; it took planning to tour that part of the world. In 2004 and 2005, we received thirty-day visas for Thailand on arrival from the USA. We bought sixty-day tourist visas for Thailand in China for twenty-five US dollars each and thirty-day tourist visas for Laos for forty-one US dollars and twenty-five cents each. We were required to buy our Chinese tourist visas in our home country (USA), the ninety-day visa cost US$130 dollars each. We bought our 180-day business visas in Beijing for US$171 each. A visa wasn't required to stay in Malaysia for fewer than ninety days. Singapore didn't require visas either.

In 2006, a one-year tourist visa for Australia, which required a chest X-ray and proof of financial assets, cost AUD$105. We received nine-month tourist visas for New Zealand after meeting the requirements of submitting a chest X-ray and showing assets of NZ$1,000 a month per person. Finally, Canada didn't require visas.

Visas can be expensive and did deter us from visiting Brazil, which at the time it cost one hundred US dollars.

BORDER CROSSINGS

Anything can happen at a border crossing. For example, a shady money changer in Guatemala rigged his calculator to show the exchange rate in his favor. When I calculated how many quetzals I should get per US dollar, it was higher compared to his. If I hadn't used my calculator, I would never have caught him.

No two border crossings were the same. Navigating from one country to the next through no man's land (sometimes over a mile – two kilometers – wide) where anything could happen, was eerie. Chaos, intimidation, and sadness come to mind when I think about the days I crossed a border.

Peru/Bolivia

October 30, 2003, our ninety-day tourist visas for Peru were running out. It was time to go to Bolivia. The Bolivian border had been closed for nearly a month by protesters, roads were blocked, and no one was going in or coming out. We wanted to cycle through Bolivia, but if the border remained closed we would have to continue south on the coast to Chile.

Farmers were protesting the eradication of coca plants (the shrub's leaves are the source of cocaine). They took to the streets in large numbers; roads were blocked with abandoned cars, boulders, and anything else that would stop the flow of traffic. Rumor had it that this was instigated by the US government, to stop the flow of cocaine to the USA.

In addition, the Bolivian president had recently proposed selling the country's natural gas to a private company and putting a pipeline through to the Chilean coast (a coast that once belonged to Bolivia, but lost to Chile in a war that ended 120 years before). The gas would be sold to Mexico and the USA. That proposal made the other half of the population angry. The people united and blocked the roads in and out of La Paz, as well. It looked like a change of plans would be necessary.

At the last minute, the protests stopped and the border was reopened. We squeezed through on the eighty-ninth day of our ninety-day tourist visas. The formalities at the border went quickly, acquiring our Peruvian exit stamp and Bolivian entrance stamp went smoothly.

On the lonely road to Copacabana, Bolivia, remnants of the battle between the farmers and the Bolivian army remained in view. At the highest pass, a burned-out car, boulders, and expended bullets littered the ground. Several brown spots that were probably dried blood stained the road. I could still feel the conflict in the air, someone may have died there days earlier. I carried this somber thought with me all the way to town where a visit to the cemetery on "Day of the Dead," or "All Saints Day," confirmed my suspicions. Farmers, who had taken up arms and protested, had lost their lives.

Thailand /Cambodia

Cambodia is one of the poorest countries in the world with a large amount of landmines.

The country was recovering from a genocide that happened during the seventies, when Pol Pot and the Khmer Rouge were in power. Pol Pot wanted an agrarian, farmer dominated society; in the transformation process he exterminated the educated population, including urban dwellers, monks, and nuns. He slaughtered twenty-five percent of the population, estimated to be two million Cambodians.

I heard from other backpackers that many people, young and old, were missing limbs. I assumed from stepping on hidden landmines. I wondered what those people would be like. *How does a country recover from genocide?* I fully expected my travels through Cambodia to be emotional, as well as physical.

Mid-December 2004, we planned to leave Thailand. Buying our visas the day before made crossing into Cambodia much easier. Border crossings always made me nervous, abrupt changes were common, and most of those changes couldn't be anticipated. I expected Aranya Pratet, Thailand to different from Poipet, Cambodia, but the difference was more extreme than I could have anticipated.

It was a dry and dusty morning. Poor road conditions on the Cambodian side threw fine silt particles into the air, creating a thick hazy sky that even the sun had trouble penetrating. Departing Thailand was painless and swift, no one else was in line. A steady stream of people dressed in shabby clothes pushed and hurried across the border into Thailand. Going the other way were the well-dressed Thai going to Poipet to gamble, mixed with smartly-dressed Cambodian girls who worked in the casinos.

As I waited for Tim at the bikes, a man in a wheelchair rolled in front of me. His legs were gone, completely gone; it made me shudder to think how he lost them. The chaos continued with little boys pulling wooden carts across the border. A legless man riding a three-wheeled machine propelled his vehicle forward by turning cranks with his hands. Another man pushed a bicycle-type machine. In place of the seat was a large basket of goods. The smells were a mixture of fish, burning garbage, and dust. Crossing into Cambodia was an intense jolt to my senses.

We stopped at the Canadia bank to change our Thai baht and US dollars to Cambodian riel. I changed the equivalent of US$200 and left the bank with a wad of cash two inches (five centimeters) thick. The exchange rate at the time (2004) was one US dollar equaled 3,960 riel. I couldn't carry that much cash around. I pulled out a few small bills, 5,000 riel from the stack, put them in my change purse, and stored the rest deep in my pannier. The average income per person in Cambodia was US$280 per year. I had practically a year's pay in my hand.

The road out of Poipet was paved for the first three miles (five kilometers), the next 6.2 miles (ten kilometers) was dirt, and the remaining 18.75 miles (thirty kilometers) to Sisophon was uneven pavement with large potholes to keep us alert. The traffic was heavy at first, then remained a steady stream the entire day. The cars were the worst for kicking up dust.

Drivers honked their horns until they passed us, so our ears were assaulted with a constant honking sound most of the day.

We began to get hungry and started looking for a place to stop, but all I saw were stands selling gasoline in every bottle imaginable. Finally, we came across a small market. We picked a table in the shade and sat down. I didn't recognize the food in the bowls on the table, except the rice. "OK, I will have two bowls of that please," I said, while pointing at what I wanted. I tried it; it was tasty like rice pudding with a few scattered beans.

As we ate, children gathered around greeting us with a welcoming "hello," and smiles. One girl, who could speak a little English, helped me pronounce a few words in Khmer, the language of Cambodia. They were all sweet children, not what I expected to find in Cambodia. For the next fifteen miles (twenty-four kilometers), the kids yelled "hello" in English and Khmer. All day I braced myself for what never happened. I had expected an emotional day of meeting desperate people and was, instead, greeted by happy, energetic children.

Singapore

Chaotic borders were the norm in southeast Asia. The Singapore border was clean, orderly, and forbidden.

September 2006 we planned to ride into Singapore over the most western bridge, Tuas Second Link, which is 6,300 feet (two kilometers) in length. Malaysian officials stamped us out and let us ride over the bridge without paying a toll. However, when we arrived at Singaporean customs and immigration, we were quickly surrounded by police and taken to an office for questioning.

They detained us (here we go again) while they tried to figure out what to do with us. The road from the customs office on Second Link to downtown was on the expressway. Bicycles were prohibited on expressways in Singapore. After much discussion, we were instructed to take the first exit and ride through Singapore on surface roads. We rode a short distance (in fear of getting fined) and got off onto a secondary road as soon as we could.

Part 4 - Stories from the Road

Priest going into a trance at the start of a Hindu fire-walking ceremony. Purit Buntar, Malaysia.

Chapter 9
What Were Your Best Bicycle Rides?

Standing in front of a termite hill in Kakadu National Park, Australia.

My favorite places to ride my bike during our around-the-world tour were the Salar de Uyuni, the world's largest salt flat, in Bolivia; going across the top of Australia, from Cairns to Kakadu National Park; and from Valdez, Alaska to Prince Rupert, Canada. All three had remoteness in common. Sometimes, we had to carry a five- to ten-day supply of food and sometimes navigated by compass. It's where I was connected to and aware of the beauty of my surroundings, including wildlife, weather, landscapes, and changing seasons.

The bonus of traveling in these out-of-the-way places was being disconnected from a phone, social media, and the Internet.

SAVANNAH WAY

We rode and camped around the eastern half of Australia from September 2006 to September 2007. Toward the end of our travels in Australia, we crossed the Outback. Based on advice from our friends from Geelong, we chose the Savannah Way as our track across the top. Our Outback adventure took us from east to west through Australia's grassy plains and monsoon woodlands on undulating roads that varied from sealed (paved) to unsealed (gravel).

Long distances between towns and scattered water sources from Cairns to Kakadu National Park required two food drops along the 1,563-mile (2,515-kilometer) route. In Cairns, I shopped, packed and shipped supplies, including peanut butter, flour for making damper bread, almonds, peanuts, ramen noodles, gummy bears, and canned meat, ahead to Wollogorang Station and Daly Waters.

While still in the planning stages of our ride across the top, I researched the best places to view wildlife and came across a small paragraph on a curtain fig tree where tree kangaroos live. I was intrigued from the beginning, what kind of tree does a tree kangaroo live in? I quickly asked Tim, "Can we detour to see where tree kangaroos live?"

"How far is the detour?" he asked.

"Not far, only twelve kilometers. We can probably find a place to camp nearby." I said.

"Sure. We can go see the tree. We're not in a rush."

"Great. I will let you know when we are close." I marked the location of the curtain fig tree, near Yungaburra, on my map.

Our plan was to head north from Cairns to Mossman, then swing back south, then west for 500 miles (805 kilometers) on the Savannah Way to Burketown via Ravenshoe, Georgetown and Normanton. Then turn off onto a more remote stretch called the Carpenteria from Burketown to Daly Waters for 560 miles (901 kilometers). At Daly Waters take the Stuart Highway north to Katherine, detour east to Kakadu, then on to Darwin.

Five days from our starting point in Cairns, we easily found the immense curtain fig tree. Fig trees grow in the opposite direction of most trees. It starts in the upper branches of a host tree and its roots grow down toward the forest floor. The host tree is eventually strangled and a hollow fig tree remains with a tangle of roots flowing to the ground.

When this particular host tree fell, it leaned on a nearby tree and the roots of the fig grew down in a curtain shape. The magnificent tree is also home to the nocturnal tree kangaroo.

We made camp just a kilometer (0.621 miles) down the road and came back after dark to look for tree kangaroos. We didn't wait long for

The magnificent curtain fig tree.

a young tree kangaroo to appear. In my excitement to get a better view, I dropped my binoculars on the platform and sent the kangaroo scurrying up the tree, not to be seen for the rest of the night. A bit disappointed (I was disappointed, but Tim wasn't), we sat for thirty minutes and took in the immensity of the 500-year-old curtain fig tree.

Back in our tent in the rainforest, as I closed my eyes to go to sleep. I felt lucky we could ride our bikes twenty thousand miles to see a tree, or a kangaroo, or a rock. We were always detouring to see something on our tour.

The first 231 miles (372 kilometers) of the Savannah Way is a two-lane road with a soft shoulder. The next section of road randomly goes from two lanes down to one. To make things interesting and dangerous, road trains, carrying ore to and from the mine at Mount Garnet, barrel up and down the road. Road trains can be four trailers, over 160 feet (fifty meters) long.

We quickly realized we needed to get off the road when both caravans (RVs) and road trains passed by. When we stayed on the road, gravel was thrown in our faces when the driver drove half on the road and half in the dirt. They barely looked in control of their vehicles, especially the caravans, when they slid sideways on the graveled shoulder. After a near miss, we changed our riding strategy to going uphill on dirt and downhill on pavement so we wouldn't come face-to-face with a vehicle at the top of a hill.

On our way to Georgetown we rode over the New Castle range, the dividing point between monsoon woodlands and the Outback. We stopped in the gateway to the Outback – Georgetown – for the night.

Gum trees, also known as eucalyptus, tall grasses, and termite mounds dot the landscape. The Outback also means crocodile (called saltys by the Aussies) country. We didn't see a salty for a few days, however, bird life was prolific.

One of the benefits of riding a bicycle is being quiet and consequently we sometimes enjoyed close encounters with wildlife. This was especially true in the Outback where a road is but a small trace through a vast wilderness.

A couple of hours outside of Georgetown, we chanced upon a large wedge-tailed eagle snacking on the latest road kill. He didn't move until we practically ran into him. Then he flew a short distance to a perch in a dead tree. I marveled at his size and beauty while he waited for us to leave so he could finish his dinner.

By the time we arrived at Gilbert River, our water source and camp for the night, it was late afternoon. We didn't have much time before sunset to get water, cook dinner, and pitch the tent. In our haste, we rode to the river to collect water. As I dipped my pan, I got a big fright when I spotted a crocodile print the size of a baseball in the sand bank next to me. I settled down quickly when I recognized the print was from a freshwater crocodile. Freshys are afraid of humans and will run away rather than attack. Still, the sight of its print in the sand got my heart thumping.

That wasn't the only thump in the Outback. The next morning I woke to a natural alarm clock that went thump, thump, thump. I bolted upright and unzipped the tent door just in time to see a mob of roos (kangaroos or possibly wallabies) hop on by. They were so close to the tent I worried they might jump in. The memory of our morning alarm clock kept a smile on my face all day.

We were now in sight of the Gulf of Carpenteria, this section of the Savannah Way runs from Normanton to Boroloola and parallels the Gulf. With few road houses to stop at, we camped free near the freshwater rivers that flowed perpendicular to the gulf. The distance between rivers averaged between thirty-eight to fifty miles (sixty-one to eighty kilometers).

At the caravan park in Normanton, a gray nomad (retiree) mentioned that a replica of the world's largest crocodile shot (by a woman) resided in town. This was something I had to see before starting my shopping and laundry chores. I walked into town in search of this great salty. Rounding the corner, I looked up the street to see a flurry of activity around the crocodile's head. As I got closer to its mouth, I witnessed a horrifying show. A couple of gray nomads had brought their small dog and placed it in the mouth of the crocodile. The terrified white poodle was shaking uncontrollably while they snapped pictures. My first instinct was to grab the dog and run. Lucky for the pooch, my presence initiated a quick release from the jaws of torture.

Caravan parks are full of gray nomads traveling the circuit around

Australia. It was a great place to exchange stories of the road; although we didn't quite fit in with the group, we joined in anyway. Information gathered at the caravan park was invaluable as we knew we would be crossing flooded causeways sometime that day. Soon after leaving Normanton we traversed two dry causeways, the Little Bynoe River and the Bynoe River. However, the Flinders River was running across the concrete causeway. I scouted up and down the river for crocodiles before I cautiously submerged my front wheel into the shallow water. The causeway was slippery, forcing me to concentrate on a steady, rather than a quick, pace across.

At the end of the day, we camped close to L-Creek and watched the prolific and diverse bird life fly by. While we set up camp, at least fifty hawks circled above. Closer to sunset, a noisy flock of little cruellas flew by.

Our ride into Burketown was a delight on a sealed (paved) road with the wind at our back. Smooth roads meant I could look around and on the way I saw wallabies hopping about and another large flock of little cruellas – 500 birds moved through the air like a wave. Their movement reminded me of a swarm of bees I once saw in Honduras. The next day, we were back to unsealed (dirt) roads as we pedaled toward our first Aboriginal town.

Domadgee has a population of 1,200 and the settlement includes a bakery, grocery store, and petrol station. Our last fully-stocked grocery store was in Atherton over 563 miles (906 kilometers) to the east. I was relieved to find most of what we needed at the grocery store. I spent over an hour restocking our supplies with oranges, bananas, oatmeal, peanut butter, biscuits (cookies), and chocolate (can't forget that) for the next leg of the trip.

The bakery was disappointing because they were out of fresh bread. At both stores I noticed most items were labeled to help diabetics make better food choices. Whole meal bread, diet cola, and soda water were labeled with a green sign, healthy, while white bread and cola were labeled with a red sign, not healthy. Obviously, the modern Australian diet is making the aboriginals sick.

On our way back to the main road, we got lost and, instead, took a tour of town. It was a dismal place; dilapidated houses with large holes in the walls were common along with people hanging around doing nothing.

Nevertheless, we were greeted by friendly people who wanted to chat.

With panniers loaded with food, we stopped at a water hole a half kilometer from Cliffdale Creek for a break, and camped the night. Our neighbors included great egrets, herons, and storks wading near shore. A family of wallabies came by for a drink at dusk. They lingered as if they were waiting to meet their new neighbors.

For dinner, I made damper bread (self-rising flour, water, and salt) for the first time. The consistency reminded me of making biscuits (not cookies) as a kid. Instead of putting the bread in aluminum foil to cook on the fire, I wrapped it around a stick and roasted it like a marshmallow. The first one was toasted on the outside and raw on the inside. The second one I cooked longer and it came out perfect. I couldn't cook them fast enough for two hungry cyclists.

The sounds of birds filled the air at dawn: hawks, sulfur-crested cockatoos, rainbow lorikeets, blue-winged kookaburras, and few more I couldn't identify. The wildlife invited us to stay another day and I leisurely took in an atmosphere of being one among many, including birds, wallabies, cows, a pair of bulls that occasionally fought in the road, and some large frogs in the creek.

Most of the next day was spent bouncing down a corrugated road, the roughest part being near the Red Bank mine. I watched Tim struggle through a sand trap, a rather large one, and I knew I had to get my speed up to get through it. My bike was bulging with food we had picked up at Wollogorang Station. I geared up, cranked on the pedals, and hit that sand trap as fast as I could. Not two bike lengths into the loose sand, I smacked a large boulder and it launched my front wheel into the air. Losing my grip on the handle bars caused my wheel to come down sideways and stick in the sand like a dart in a board. All my momentum had to go somewhere, so I was launched over the handlebars and landed in the dirt in front of my bike with a thud and a groan.

Groans always feel better when you can lie on the ground and soak them in.

I didn't get the chance. A car was coming down the completely empty, until I messed up, road. I quickly jumped up and dragged my bike out of the middle of the road. The car slowed, the driver rolled down his window and said, "What are you doing on this road?"

This took me by surprise and I said, "I am riding through the Outback. I was doing fine until a minute ago."

He said, "Yeah, OK," as if to imply I was lying and drove on by. He never did ask me if I was all right, the yahoo. Thinking back, he may have suspected I was investigating the nearby mine that had copper-green water draining from it and most likely contaminating the local water supply.

My body was ready for a rest day at the caravan park in Borroloola (I loved that name). We must have looked hungry, because the campers to our left cooked us breakfast of eggs and toast, then, in the evening, the campers to our right fed us steak and pasta.

We were off to a mid-morning start when Tim noticed his Brooks saddle was hanging on by a thread. Ugh. It would have been nice if he had noticed it on our day off. Brooks saddle is an old style English saddle, a piece of leather stretched between the rails of the seat. It was the leather that was pulling away from the nose of Tim's seat. The closest store didn't have any Super Glue™. We could take off and hope it lasted or turn around, go back into town, and buy Super Glue™ at the other store, 1.25 miles (two kilometers) in the wrong direction. We turned around, bought Super Glue™, and waited half an hour for it to dry.

In the meantime, we had an opportunity to talk with a few of the aboriginal elders in town. I wish we had had more time to chat. So, we didn't push off down the road until 10 a.m. Ouch. We had seventy-five miles (121 kilometers) to ride. At least the terrain was flat most of the day and as we steadily turned west we had more and more of a tailwind. We arrived at Heartbreak Hotel too early for dinner and too late for lunch. So it was a beer until dinner was served.

My legs were tired from the long ride to Heartbreak Hotel. It didn't help that the terrain had changed to undulating with a medium climb of 492 feet (150 meters). Not a big climb, but we were beginning to feel the change in heat and humidity. Until Borroloola a couple of days earlier, it had been warm during the day and cool to cold at night. We could ride all day long. The higher temperatures now forced us to take more breaks. We pulled into a rest area at the top of the hill. A nice view greeted us in all directions and, with the addition of shade and a water tank, we considered stopping. After a discussion about how much food we had, and a review of our schedule, we called it a day and stayed the night. We thought we had the place to ourselves until 5 p.m. when all the caravaners came roaring in, five in all, plus a huge bus. Howdy neighbors. Turned out everyone was friendly, which was always the case in Australia. That was a whole lot better than some foreigners who pretended we didn't exist.

Daly Waters is a famous roadhouse on the Stuart Highway. It had a reputation for having a good restaurant, caravan park, and post office. It was our second food drop on our way to Darwin. Tired and ready to eat, we collected our food box from the post office. The young woman behind the counter wouldn't look me in the eye as she slid my package over; it was open and half the contents had been removed.

I was shocked and weak in the knees from hunger. Everything that didn't need cooking had been removed. I returned to our campsite depleted of energy, our neighbors gave us a couple of power bars that prevented me from going into a sugar melt down. Daly Waters wasn't what the guidebooks said it was anymore. An overcrowded caravan park had over-taxed the septic system and it was overflowing. Our planned rest day was aborted and we left the next morning.

The beauty of always being on the move was that nothing stayed the same. The next day we rode to Green Park and took a rest day. It was more like being at a farm than a caravan park. Ben and Di, who have a passion for animals and took in injured wildlife, had a large family: a resident potbellied pig, two cows, a water buffalo and her six-month-old, a freshy crocodile, a bird aviary with a few kinds of parrots, a couple of guinea pigs, and last, but not least, a baby gray kangaroo.

The four-month-old baby kangaroo had been rescued by an American family in west Australia. By the time they reached Green Park in the Northern Territory, it was dying. Ben and Di took over its care. They kept it in a bag (because it resembled a pouch) and hung it by the freezer where it was warm. At four months, it barely hopped. When feeding time came around I was lucky he didn't mind a newcomer. Feeding him was like feeding a baby and such big brown eyes, too. I was love struck.

I could have stayed a week at Green Park, but we had to keep moving, our visas were ending soon and we wanted to get to Kakadu. It was a five-day ride from Green Park to Kakadu and with each passing day it became hotter and more humid.

As we approached Kakadu we saw a group of brumbies (wild horses) through the bush, one stallion and three mares. A little farther down the road we crossed a river and looked down and saw a freshy crocodile. When my shadow hit the water, he swam to the deep end of the pool to hide in the mud. Then at lunch, we saw two water buffalos wandering near a creek. The brumbies and water buffalos are feral (domesticated animals that are wild), but it's the park's policy not to cull them. Kakadu had plenty of wildlife to see.

While staying at a caravan park in Cooinda, we ventured deeper into the wilderness. The morning cruise on Yellow Water Billabong started before dawn. Our boat wasn't full, so I could wander from side to side during the trip. Right off the dock was a big salty, over eight feet (two and a half meters) long, most of her was underwater.

At first the billabongs (seasonal waterways) were quiet and covered in mist. As the bright orange sun shone through at dawn, everyone woke up: the birds, the crocs, and the horses. It was so beautiful, the symphony of sound combined with fresh morning movement of wildlife, stirred my sense of admiration for Mother Nature. We cruised out of the billabong and into the East Alligator River.

As we turned westward into another waterway, I heard something slapping the water. I raised my binoculars to my eyes expecting to see a crocodile. Instead, I saw an aboriginal woman collecting reeds from the edge of the waterway. She was chest deep in water. My heart skipped a beat as I blurted out, "Oh. No." The woman driving the boat shushed me and explained that the aboriginals are taught from a young age how to collect those reeds. Relieved, I went back to viewing the many birds in the tree tops.

Kakadu is next to Arnhem Land, aboriginal land that a permit is required to visit. We were in luck. The one day a year it is open to the public – August 17 – we were at Kakadu. We took the day to visit Oenpelli (Gunbalunya) to watch basket-weaving, painting, and a footie (Australian rules football) game.

We returned to Merl Campground expecting to continue on toward Darwin the next day.

Chapter 10
What Were Your Favorite Places?

Machu Picchu, Peru.

Besides pedaling through remote areas of the world, I enjoyed visiting the greatest civilizations of our past, including Palenque, a Mayan city in Mexico that flourished from 226 BC to around 799 AD; Machu Picchu, an Inca city in Peru that thrived for nearly a hundred years from 1450 AD until it was abandoned after the Spanish Conquest; and Angkor Wat (the largest religious monument in the world), a Khmer city in Cambodia built in the early 1200s. These lost or ancient civilizations were amazing to see, but they also have a message, more along the lines of a warning. *The question is – are we listening?*

PALENQUE – MEXICO

The Mayan ruins of Palenque are located on the foothills of eastern Chiapas where the mountains meet the plains of the Yucatan Peninsula. The ruins lie within a steamy hot jungle, making it not an easy place to get to by bicycle. I remember overheating on the way into the city of Palenque and waking up the next morning with a heat stress-induced headache. Still, this didn't deter me from wanting to explore these famous ruins that were designated an UNESCO Heritage site in 1987.

The Mayans, who built and lived in the city, called it "Lakham Ha," meaning "Big Water." When the ruins were discovered by Fray Pedro Lorenzo de la Nada in 1567, the locals called it "Otolum," meaning "strong house land" or "fortified houses." Thus, it was translated to "Palenque" in Spanish.

To be closer to Palenque, we camped at the Maya Bell campground within walking distance from the temples. Rather than go through the main entrance, the way most tourists do, our weekly pass allowed us to stroll in the back way with the locals. This approach took us past many pools, streams, and cascading waterfalls that lined the northern side of the excavated area. Before we even saw the structural remains left behind by the great Mayan architects, we were shown the reason a city of 70,000 people lived there. Plenty of water for the inhabitants to drink and, at times, so much water the flow through the city was managed by canals and aqueducts.

Palenque was founded at the beginning of the Christian era or Late Preclassic and peaked in art and architecture around 500 AD. Over 1,400 structures occupy roughly five square miles (eight square kilometers) of which ten percent of the buildings have been excavated. The ruins are constructed of limestone giving the temples a white to gray color, but at the time of occupation they were bright red.

In the early morning, we entered the main exhumed area from the north. Our first view of the Great Plaza, still immersed in fog, took my breath away. The Plaza is dominated by the Palace. To the west of the Palace, lined up along the southern side of a large promenade, are the Temple of Inscriptions, Temple XIII (Red Queen), Temple of the Skull, and Temple XII. This is also where the main entrance to Palenque is located.

The Palace is the largest structure of the group and is comprised of buildings, courtyards, and ceremonial baths. The four-story observation tower on the southwestern side of the complex was built for viewing the winter solstice and still had small trees sprouting from the top. The Mayan architects had developed the corbel arch giving their buildings long narrow walkways surrounding an inner courtyard. This courtyard was filled with frescos and large carvings of the rulers of Palenque.

The Temple of Inscriptions is the most well-known structure of the group and is the burial ground of Palenque's most admired ruler, Kinich Janaab Pakal. Even in ancient times, the Temple of Inscriptions was famous and many people came to pay homage to the great leader who ruled for sixty-eight years (age twelve to eighty) and was responsible for the construction of some of Palenque's surviving monuments. At the time of our October 2002 visit, the Temple of Inscriptions was closed for renovations and the museum was under construction. So I still don't know the answer to this question.

My body was adjusting to the hot and humid climate; the slightest exertion induced buckets of sweat to empty from every pore in my body. Over a week's time, we made the daily trek into the ruins exploring as many restored temples and unrestored mounds that we could. The jungle had overtaken ninety percent of the complex and large trees could be seen growing out of numerous stairways to unexcavated temples. This gave the feeling that the stairways were endless, because the tops were shrouded in vegetation. We soon learned that it was much cooler to be on top of the temples where we could get a breeze than down in the steamy jungle. I wondered if this was the reason the temples were built – to get away from the stifling heat from the jungle below – or were they used as lookouts to monitor the movements of their rivals on the plains below? Perhaps both?

My favorite group of temples, Group of the Cross, is located a short distance to the south of the Palace. Our final morning there was spent inside the Temple of Cruz Foliaga. I perused stone carvings of Pakal and his son, Chan Bahlum. The intricate nature of the carvings drew me in to inspect every detail; I could still see the outline of their finger nails. The date was recorded with Mayan hieroglyphics, if only I could decipher the code. That afternoon, I gazed at the view of the Grand Plaza and the plains beyond from outside the Temple of Cruz Foliada for more than an hour.

After nearly a week, it was time to leave the ruins. I was a little sad because I would miss exploring the many wonders of this ancient place with beautiful architecture and intricate art. Lost in these thoughts, I wasn't paying attention to where I was going as I walked down a set of stairs near the Temple of Inscriptions. Suddenly, my foot came down sideways on an odd-shaped step. Before pain penetrated my thoughts, the sound of my ankle tendon snapping ripped through my ears. In disbelief, I looked down to see my ankle swell into a knot in seconds. In a bit of a shocked state, I limped down the remaining steps and over to the food stands where Tim got a big chunk of ice to reduce the swelling. By then the pain had kicked in, my adrenaline shot up, and my blood sugar dropped rapidly. While sitting beside a vendor, icing my ankle, tears streamed uncontrollably. The woman who gave Tim the ice came over and tenderly checked my ankle. I could tell she had examined sprained ankles before. She patted my arm to tell me I was OK and gave me a couple of bananas. I was humbled by this sweet gesture. Eating the banana stabilized my blood sugar, my weepy tears were gone, and I knew it was time to leave.

I could have taken a cab down the hill to the Maya Bell, but I couldn't bear the thought of leaving the ruins by taxi. I had spent days trekking up and down the steep temple steps, this was no time to get lazy. With Tim's help, we slowly walked down the local's trail through the jungle. As we descended between two unexcavated mounds, I glanced down to see a piece of building block on its side. Facing upward toward me were the most beautifully preserved hieroglyphs. A perfect place to sit, rest, and inspect the fine carvings. I wondered what message it had for the person who could decipher the code. It was time to go. I still needed to get past the springs, waterfalls, and pools. My last stop at Palenque was at one of the pools to soak my ankle in its cooling water.

ANGKOR WAT – CAMBODIA

The Khmer ruins of Angkor Wat are in the province of Siem Reap, located in north central Cambodia. The climate is tropical. Peak dry season with pleasant temperatures is from November through February, the hottest part of the dry season being March through May, and rainy season is June through October. The closest place to stay is Siem Reap, four miles (six kilometers) away. It hosts a full range of accommodations from backpacker guesthouses to five-star hotels.

The terrain is flat, making it an ideal place to ride a bicycle. I highly recommend viewing the ruins by bicycle, which will give you the freedom to explore the temples at your leisure and avoid the large tour groups hopping from one monument to the next. For those enthusiastic explorers, viewing Angkor Wat at sunrise is magical.

Angkor Archaeological Park covers more than 240 square miles (385 square kilometers) and includes the Temple of Angkor Wat, the city complex of Angkor Thom with the Bayon Temple, Ta Prom, and Preah Khan, and many other outer ruins. The park was classified a UNESCO Heritage site in 1992.

Construction of Angkor Wat, meaning "City of Temples," began in the twelfth century by Suryavarman II as the state temple and capital city. This Hindu temple was built as a dedication to the god Vishnu and differs from earlier state temples built by preceding rulers in that it faces west rather than east. The buildings are constructed from sandstone quarried from fifteen miles (twenty-four kilometers) away. Hauling the large tonnage of stone to Angkor via the river Siem Reap is on the same magnitude as the movement of stone to the Great Pyramids of Egypt.

The Angkor complex is surrounded by a thirteen-foot (four-meter) deep, 650-foot (200-meter) wide moat that most likely prevented it from being overtaken by the surrounding jungle. The water-enclosed temple represents Mount Meru, a mythical mountain at the center of Hinduism, Buddhism, and Jainism that is supposedly located between the realm of humans and the gods.

The interior walls are decorated with apsaras (celestial dancing girls) and bas-reliefs that narrate current events of the time, such as the court and procession of Suryavarman II, builder of the complex, and the mythological Hindu tale of the "Churning of the Ocean of Milk."

Other complexes we explored were Angkor Thom with the Buddhist Bayon Temple, Ta Phrom, made famous by the movie, *Laura Croft: Tomb Raider* and Preah Khan (Sacred Sword).

Angkor Thom, meaning "Great City," and the Bayon Temple are located approximately one mile (one and a half kilometers) to the north of Angkor Wat. They were built in the early part of the twelfth century, after the Angkor Wat complex, by King Jayavarman VII, a Mahayana Buddhist.

We entered the complex by crossing a causeway over a now extinct moat. Lining each side of the causeway is a row of devas (a superhuman being in Buddhism or a supernatural entity in Hinduism) on the left and a row of asuras (power-seeking deities and usually found in battle with the devas) on the right. As we rode through the south gate we got our first glimpse at the face of Avalokitesvara (the Buddhist deity of compassion) who gazed down on us as we proceeded through the entrance. The first temple we found, Bayon, was the state temple for King Jayavarman VII. It didn't appear to be much from afar, but as we approached we could see the many faces of Avalokitesvara all serenely looking down at us from the third level of Bayon.

There are over two hundred faces within the Bayon temple complex and some scholars say that the large carvings have a striking resemblance to King Jayavarman VII, who may have been a bodhisattva (an enlightened being).

On the first level, along the southern wall, are detailed bas-reliefs carved from sandstone. Narrations on the wall depict historical events and everyday life of the local Khmer, as well as Buddhist symbols, including apsaras.

Located north of Bayon is the Terrace of the Elephants, which was most likely a viewing platform for the royals, and Temple of the Leper King, possibly a monument to a king who died of leprosy.

The Temple Ta Prohm, or 'Old Brahma," made famous by the *Laura Croft: Tomb Raider* movie is more magical in real life than any film or photo can capture. Located to the east of Angkor Thom and northeast of Angkor Wat, it is easy to take in while viewing the other major temples of Angkor Wat. Ta Prohm is part of the larger Mahayana Buddhist complex built by King Jayavarman VII that includes his capital city of Angkor Thom, the temples of Banteay Kdei, Preah Khan, and hundreds of others.

Temple records show that Ta Prohm was a royal monastery that housed over 12,500 monastics, at least eighteen high priests and 615 dancers, with more than 80,000 people living around the monastery.

Built in 1186 AD, as a dedication to King Jayavarman VII's mother, the monastery became extremely wealthy over time and once stored vast riches in gold, jewels, and silk. When the king died, so did the conversion to Mahayana Buddhism. Most of the Buddhist images in all the temples he built were destroyed when the Angkor Empire returned to Hinduism with King Jayavarman VIII.

Ta Prohm has been looted over the centuries with all the riches removed and a substantial amount of bas-reliefs defaced, as well. What remains has been kept in place by the encroachment of the jungle. A large complex with many dark hallways and Buddhist offering sites scattered throughout make it an inspiring complex to explore.

MACHU PICCHU – PERU

The Inca ruins of Machu Piccu are perched on a peak that is estimated to be 7,970 feet (2,400 meters) above the Urubamba River below. It was built around 1450 AD during the height of the Inca Empire by the two great Inca emperors: Pachacutec Inca Yupanqui (1438-71) and Tupac Inca Yupanqui (1472-93).

The site was abandoned in the sixteenth century when the Spanish Conquistadors conquered the Inca Empire. The Spaniards quest for gold and riches led them throughout the Inca Empire, but somehow they didn't find the city. The city lay dormant for centuries until it was discovered in 1911 by Hiram Bingham, of Yale University. Bingham wrote a few books on Machu Picchu, including *The Lost City of the Incas*.

No one knows for sure the exact function of the city that supported possibly more than 100,000 people.

Some of the major features of the site include Temple of the Sun, Water Canals, Storage Area, Terraced Fields, Common Area, Sacred Rock, and Inca Bridge, to name a few.

THE UPS AND DOWNS OF EMPIRES

Of the three empires, Machu Picchu was the shortest lived, stopped abruptly by war, and has the least amount of information presented at the site. To my disappointment, there was no museum, gift shop, or even a map available. To get an understanding of what we were viewing we brought our guidebook map with us.

I was hesitant to hire a tour guide for good reasons; they don't know what is going on and they make up stories. I heard numerous versions of those stories the day we toured Machu Picchu, ranging from the site was for women only, to virgins were sacrificed often, to it was home to the king in the summer and reserved for the religious elite. The last speculation is probably closer to the truth, but without a museum to display artifacts, and update new findings, anything could be true.

Palenque was the longest inhabited site and to my knowledge studied the most. Palenque's downfall came at the hands of war and the depletion of natural resources. Twenty years ago we didn't know what the hieroglyphics in the temples meant, but archeologists are making advancements in deciphering those glyphs. At the time I visited Palenque the museum was being built to house artifacts found at the site. This reason alone would inspire me to return. This, combined with the opening of the Temple of Inscriptions, puts this site as a must visit for me in the future.

Of the three countries, Mexico has the best policy of opening its historical sites and museums to everyone on Sundays. Locals and backpackers on a budget can visit these sites for free. This is in contrast to Machu Picchu and Angkor Wat where the fees to visit are far out of reach for locals.

Angkor Wat, in Cambodia, is the largest religious monument in the world. Recent satellite data reveals more than one million people lived around the state temples that thrived between the twelfth and fifteenth centuries. An elaborate irrigation system crisscrosses the site and water was used to sustain life, grow crops, clean temples, move stone from quarries to the temples, and provide protection as a moat around the famous Angkor Wat complex. The demise of the large complex is mostly attributed to the overuse of resources.

All three empires fell due to conflict, war, and depletion of natural resources. These sites show that it is only a matter of time before modern empires, whereever they may be, will most likely fall due to the same reasons.

Chapter 11
Who Are the People You Remember Most?

At Maria's home near Quetzaltenango, Guatemala.

Meeting thousands of people over the years, I have to say no two were alike. We all have similar traits, but the beauty of being human is being different, yet the same.

As I recounted the memorable people I met, most were men, few were women. Then I considered how I met people and realized, in most parts of the world, woman are not alone. When I did meet one they were usually with their sister, mother, husband, brother, uncle, or father. Knowing this, I realized that Maria in Guatemala was an exception.

MARIA IN GUATEMALA

December 2002, on our way to Quetzaltenango, Guatemala, we camped in a nice pine forest more than 160 feet (fifty meters) from the road. While relaxing and enjoying the sunset, an old man with five children walked into our camp. Grandfather was nervous about our presence and told us it was dangerous to camp near the road because of bandits. Soon after, he walked to his village with the children following him. His anxious behavior and warning put us in a state of panic.

We thought we were far enough from the road to not be seen, but now we were uncertain. Tim and I stayed awake all night listening for any movement in the forest. I jumped at the slightest sound in the bushes. In the morning, I was groggy but thankful an uneventful night had passed.

While enjoying our morning coffee, a group of women collecting pine needles wandered close to our camp. "Ola. Buenas dias," I said in a friendly tone.

"Ola. Mi nombre es Maria," the closest woman to me said without any hesitation. Maria was gathering pine needles in a pile while she talked to me. Her timid demeanor was mixed with friendliness and a tinge of curiosity. Her unassuming nature pulled me in and I got up from my seat to stand closer to her. I was a foot (0.305 meters) taller than the woman who looked to be in her mid-twenties. Her dark black hair was pulled back at the base of her neck and her high cheekbones suggested she was of Mayan decent. She then invited us to lunch at her home. An invitation we couldn't refuse.

Home was a couple of kilometers away and down a steep slippery hill. Down is always easier than up on a loaded bike. I knew returning to the highway would be a challenge. Well, we could worry about this later.

We arrived in a small village populated by mostly women and a few old men. I assumed the men were working in the fields. One older gentleman asked Tim if we had brought Bibles with us. Obviously, we weren't the first foreigners to visit his village.

Maria's home was modest, two rooms made of adobe walls, a dirt floor, a tin roof, and no electricity or running water. Heat was provided by a kiln-like stove in one of the rooms. The backyard, where we sat, was surrounded by cornstalks now drying in the autumn air. A fresh crop of beans was whirling its way up and around the brittle cornstalks.

Maria introduced us to the rest of her family: five women, and three children. Of the five women, only Maria could speak Spanish. Rather than just sit and chat, Maria embroidered a new blouse and talked. I watched her hand the blouse to a woman next to her who continued the embroidering as Maria brought us lunch. Another woman continued working on the blouse when the first one tended to a baby.

Lunch was a cup of blended boiled corn, attole. As I took my first sip of the bitter drink, I prayed it was boiled long enough so I wouldn't get sick. I wasn't about to decline her generous offer of attole and freshly roasted corn. We finished lunch and the extent of my Spanish about the same time. We thanked Maria for her kindness and said our good-byes to the rest of the family. I was dreading tackling the slippery slope back to the highway, but at least I would be doing it on a full stomach.

LUCHO IN PERU

Chino, whom we met in Puerto Chicama, gave us the name of a person we could stay with in Trujillo, a place where traveling cyclists stopped for rest. Luis Alberto Ramirez D'Angelo (Lucho), along with his wife, Araceli, and daughter, Angela, and young Luis Alberto Ramirez D'Angelo (he wasn't born yet when we were there), took in cyclists and in return asked for a donation or assistance around the house. In 2003 Lucho had been taking in cyclists for more than ten years; the last I checked (2014) he had just hosted his 2,000th cyclist.

Arriving at Lucho's felt like letting the air out of an over-pressurized tire. Our escort from a bicycle shop, where we had asked for directions, led us through meandering, car-choked streets. He left us at a door with a painting above it – a racing cyclist on one side, a touring cyclist on the other side, both held a globe of the world in their hands. As I admired the painting, the door below opened and we were pulled inside. The door was quickly shut behind us, then two locks and a latch were closed. We stood in a large room still holding onto our fully-loaded touring bicycles.

The front room was covered with posters of racing cyclists and, in the back corner, where Lucho stood, was a bike shop where repairs could be made. We were introduced to the family and two cyclists with their dog. They invited us to sit and relax. Our initial plan was to stay for three days but we stayed for seven. While there, I reviewed maps and route descriptions from other cyclists, visited Chan Chan (Chimú and Moche ruins) by bicycle with Lucho, Angela, Tim and Fritz, and visited the Temple of the Moon and Sun (Moche ruins) with Araceli.

Araceli baked flan and meringue, strawberry and custard pies to sell at the market across the street. Of course, I had to try every one. I couldn't decide on my favorite; they were all good.

A German cyclist named Fritz was riding the same direction to

Huarez; we three left the following Tuesday. Lucho rode with us to Viru where we had lunch. Afterward, he turned back toward Trujillo while we continued on to Chao. As I waved good-bye to Lucho, I wondered how many other cyclists he had escorted to the outskirts of town.

Lucho's was a unique place for cyclists; we didn't find anything like it until years (2006) later in Malaysia.

DAVID IN MALAYSIA

Toward the end of our twenty-two-month tour of Southeast Asia we entered Malaysia, my first Muslim country. I had no idea what to expect. Malaysians follow a mix of religions with more than sixty-one percent of the population practicing Islam, nearly twenty percent are Buddhists, almost ten percent are Christian, and over six percent are Hindus. This mixture of religion and culture came to life while staying with a fellow cyclist named David.

We had met in Siem Reap, Cambodia, over a year and four months earlier. David is of Tamil Indian decent and an avid bike tourist. His guesthouse is in Parit Buntar, twenty-eight miles (forty-five kilometers) from Butterworth. I think of his place as a Cyclist House (similar Lucho's place) because most of his guests are cyclists.

We had already met David, so we didn't fear his intentions; we knew he was genuine.

However, it was a little unnerving to walk into his living room and see our wedding picture (Tim and I getting married on bikes), from Las Vegas, on the wall with the rest of his family photos. He knew more about our travels than most people, consequently, he was more familiar with us than we were with him.

While looking through photos of cyclists, I asked, "David, how do you meet so many cyclists?"

"I ride my scooter up and down the main road going to Kuala Lumpur looking for bike tourists to invite in," he replied.

"Really?"

"Yes, I stop them and ask if they want to stay at my house," he answered.

"Do they come with you?" I asked, while thinking probably not.

"Some, but most don't," he said sadly. I wasn't surprised that most declined.

"David, you are scaring the daylights out of those cyclists, especially the young ones. They don't know what your intentions are so they run away," I said.

"What should I say first?" he asked.

"Tell them you are a touring cyclist, too, and you have a guesthouse where many cyclists have stayed," I recommended.

"I will try that next," he said.

By the time we reached David's place we had been cycling for more than seventeen months in Asia. Worn out from traveling, we looked for a place to relax, and work on an audiobook and our next book (this took relaxing completely out of the equation). The Cameron Highlands fit our needs nicely; it's a former British hill station above the heat of the tropics (we weren't that far from the equator) where the temperatures and humidity were beginning to get unbearable.

David helped us plan our two-month stay in the Cameron Highlands. We left our bikes and nonessential gear with him and took the bus to the village of Cameron.

After ten weeks there, we came down from our perch and stayed with David for what started out as one week and morphed into three.

While at David's we went to a Hindu wedding, fire-walking ceremony, Chinese opera, Chinese Ghost Month festival, saw a man stand on a sword while in a trance, visited a Buddhist temple with a life size rendering of hell, a pottery shed, a toddy plantation, and a Chinese funeral.

David, the local electrician, knew everyone and everyone knew David. He spoke four languages: Tamil, Malay (a native Muslim dialect), a Chinese dialect, and English. Everyone's hospitality was a result of him repairing their electricity when it went out.

I think he likes people and is a born tour guide. If there were more people in this world like David, we wouldn't have so many misunderstandings. He glided between cultures like a warm knife through butter.

David still takes in cyclists with probably more than two hundred have stayed with him. I feel lucky to have had the opportunity to spend time with him and his large family.

A monk recieving alms (sticky rice) early in the morning in Luang Phrabang, Laos.

Chapter 12
What Were Your Favorite Parts of the Journey?

These women invited us to have breakfast with them in their home.

Some people eat to survive while some survive to eat. I fall in the latter category. My most vivid memories from years on my bike have to do with food, the "carrot" that kept me going on the trip. I am biased when I think back about the countries I traveled through – good food equals good country. I realized early on that if the food was good, I was happy. If the food wasn't so good, I trudged on. It was amazing how much delight I got from finding a good restaurant or cook.

FOOD

In my opinion, Mexico has some of the best food in the world. It changes from chili rellenos in the north to garlic shrimp on the coast to chicken mole in the east. The locals always took pride in what they served in their restaurants and sometimes their homes.

One morning we arrived in a town in northern Mexico called Bachiniva in search of a restaurant. I asked the first woman I saw, "Is there a restaurant in town?"

"I know where you can eat. Follow me," she replied.

We followed her a short distance down the cobblestone street. Then she disappeared down a flight of stairs that ended at someone's home. I quickly followed behind her and found myself standing in a brightly lit kitchen with three women sitting at a table and a fourth by a stove. When I realized I wasn't in a restaurant, but someone's house, I turned to leave.

"Sorry, I thought this was a restaurant," I said to the elderly woman standing next to the stove.

"Sit. Sit. We will feed you," she said.

My empty stomach that had begun grumbling a half hour before couldn't disagree. Tim and I were told not to worry about our bikes and were escorted to sit at the table. Coffee was poured and tortillas flew off the griddle and onto my plate. There's nothing like the smell of a warm tortilla. Now to add some butter, roll it up, and eat. The next dish offered to us was sweet smelling chili rellenos; my favorite Mexican meal (could be my all-time favorite).

Chili rellenos are plabano peppers stuffed with cheese and, in this case, cheese and potatoes. The chili is then dipped in egg, or an egg and flour batter and fried. The smell of roasting chilis intoxicates me, like the smell of sweet tobacco to an ex-smoker (that's me, too). While sitting in that cozy room, the smell of chili rellenos entered my nostrils and took over my brain function like a drug. I was rooted to the chair. After two steaming plates of chili rellenos and beans, my stomach was quieted and in its place was a contented one.

I tried to pay for our mouthwatering breakfast, but they refused our money. The woman who brought us to the kitchen responded with, "Con mucho gusto," literally, "with much pleasure."

"Con mucho gusto tambien," I responded.

FAVORITE FESTIVALS

Humans are a festive bunch and if we have an opportunity to socialize, eat, perform rituals, plays, or dances, we do. By far, these events were the most interesting to me simply because of their diversity and historical significance. Whenever we happened upon a cultural event we stayed to experience it.

Alms Luang Prabang

We landed in Luang Prabang (once the capital city of Laos) late in the day. It was New Year's Eve 2005 and finding a vacant room was a challenge. Soon after settling in we met a Swiss, named Lars, and two of his friends having a beer on the guesthouse balcony. When Lars asked if we wanted to go with him to see alms the next morning, we quickly agreed. Not wanting to appear uninformed, in a low whisper I asked, "What is alms?"

Lars chuckled, gave me a warm smile, and said, "Alms is when the monks are given their daily food by devout pilgrims."

"Why do they do that?" I asked.

"It is a sign of respect from a lay person (someone who hasn't taken vows) to a monk, someone who has taken vows." The local people believe that by giving sticky rice to monks, they in turn will receive good merit for their generosity."

"I see," I replied, still not understanding what he meant by good merit and why you would want it.

When we stepped out to the street the next morning it was still dark. Damp air hung heavy with moisture, as it always does just before sunrise. I enjoyed the morning silence as I took in a deep breath. As I breathed out, I relaxed and contemplated what it would be like to be a nun, to give up all my worldly possessions and study Buddhism. It seemed like a huge sacrifice to me, but I didn't know much about Buddhism.

As we walked up the street, I could see the saffron robes of the monks (I didn't see any nuns) glowing in the morning light. Everything around them was dull in comparison. The monks stood in a line that extended around the block. The young monk in front of me looked to be about eight years old. His head was freshly shaved, his saffron robe was tied at the waist with a golden yellow belt, and he was barefoot. In his hands was a brass colored bowl supported by a homemade woven strap. This is the alms bowl that sticky rice is placed into.

Pilgrims, who lined the street, knelt on bamboo mats or rugs, removed cubes of sticky rice from a bamboo container, placed one in each monk's bowl as they passed. Most of the pilgrims were Asian, but I did see a few westerners giving rice, as well. We stood at the end of the line and by the time the monks got to us their bowls overflowed.

I watched a monk step out of line and give a small boy with a basket in his hands some of his rice. The boy held the basket so low that a street dog came over and helped himself to a few cubes. This sent the child and the monk into a fit of laughter. I had to smile; no one was going home hungry that day.

Festival Thai Sangkran

Thailand is a Buddhist country known as the "land of many smiles." True to their reputation, I saw many smiles in Thailand. They are people who enjoy having fun and the Thai festival of Songkran is a time for fun and celebration of the New Year. The term Songkran comes from Sanskrit "Sankranta" and means "a move or change," when entering a New Year. Traditionally, images of Buddha at all wats (temples) throughout Thailand were bathed by gently pouring water over them, that water was considered to be blessed and was thrown on people at the temples for good luck and prosperity. That tradition has since spilled out onto the streets and turned into full-blown water battles, with large quantities of water thrown at whomever comes near the festivities.

We arrived during Songkran, and knew we would be targets on our bikes, but we agreed the night before, *hey this will be fun*. With temperatures at 40° C, (103° F) it was the hottest time of year. The first bucket of water landed on Tim around 10 a.m. Others continued until we arrived in the city of Trang some five hours later. Riding past groups of Thais armed with cooling water and talc powder was a delight at first. However, as it got later in the day, the road blocks grew larger and the participants rowdier and rowdier. By the end of the day I was happy to hide in a hotel room.

Fire-walking in Malaysia

While in Malaysia we stayed with another cyclist, David, (See David in Malaysia, page 67). David introduced us to many festivals in the diverse country of Malaysia where Hindus, Buddhists, Christians, and Muslims live together.

We were in luck. The Hindu temple within walking distance from David's house was preparing for a fire-walking ceremony. My first thought was, *Why would anyone walk across hot coals?* It didn't take long to learn the answer.

The decision to participate in a fire-walking ceremony comes from taking vows. In the Hindu religion, a person can take vows on their own behalf, or on another person's behalf, promising that if illness or misfortune is averted or overcome, or success is achieved, they (it also can be the person for whom the vow was taken) will walk across the fire. Dire consequences are believed to follow for breaking such a vow.

Walking on fire requires preparation: for three to seven days prior to walking on hot coals a strict no meat or alcohol diet is followed. In addition, the devotee must sleep alone on the floor for at least three days (I think this is a polite way of saying no sex before the ceremony) to reach a state of purity.

On the day of the ceremony we went to the main temple and had lunch with a large group of Tamil Indians. Then we followed the crowd back to the palm oil plantation where the snake (Naga) god temple is located. As we followed the mass of devotees to the ceremonial grounds, the sound of repetitive drumming pierced the silence of the palm forest. Near the smaller Naga temple, I heard low moaning intermingled with drumming. I was drawn to a group of men gathered around someone on the ground. As I peered over the shoulder of a man in front of me, a withering dark back belonging to a young man came into view. He was moaning and convulsing as another man pierced his skin with one large hook after another.

I about fainted when I connected with how much pain this man must be in. An older man standing next to me exclaimed in English, "He is showing gratitude to the goddess Draupadi."

"Oh. Do the hooks have to be that big?" I asked.

"The bigger the hook the more gratitude, madam," he proclaimed.

"Do women show their gratitude this way?"

"No, madam. They go into a trance like those women over there." He pointed to a group dressed in yellow sarees with green garlands around their necks.

"Oh, I think I prefer the trance to the hooks," I announced.

"Yes, I know madam. You are a woman."

I smiled at the man and strolled over to see what was going on with the women.

As I scanned the group in a trance I saw one woman with a small spear threaded through her face. It pierced just below her lower lip, came out her mouth, and then pierced the inside of her left nostril, and came out the other side of her nose. She didn't appear to be in pain; she had a zombie-like look on her face. What amazed me was she remained in her trance until the completion of the fire-walking ceremony some five hours later. This was probably for the best, because eating was out of the question while wearing that ornament. I wondered if any of my body-pierced family or friends back home would be up for a ceremony like this.

I made my way to the Naga mound that looked like a termite hill with yellow ribbons wrapped around it. I watched the ceremonial priest dance around the mound and chant himself into a trance. I was mesmerized by his transformation from an ordinary person to the priest in charge of the festival. He held a small drum which he beat to match the rhythm of his mantra. He, too, remained in a trance for over five hours.

Meanwhile, the two young men who had large hooks piercing their skin down both sides of their spine, walked by. It was now obvious what the hooks were for. Tied to each hook was a strap. Another man, possibly a friend, held the reins while the man with the mutilated back pulled on them. They were held in a similar manner to pulling on the reins of a horse. The men slowly marched from the Naga ceremonial grounds at the palm oil plantation to the main temple located 1.25 miles (two kilometers) away. Behind them, more than one hundred devotees made their way to the fire pit, as well. Three men beat drums and sounded horns in a rhythm that mesmerized everyone, the pied pipers of the group led the way to the main temple.

The fire pit was ready. The priest walked over the freshly raked glowing coals twice before taking his position at the front of the pit. Devotees lined up to take their turn crossing the coals. Once at the front, the priest checked to see if the devotee was ready to walk over the coals. How he knew this was a mystery to me. If the devotee was ready, he instructed them to first walk through a pool of water, and then over the coals. If the devotee was not ready, he or she was instructed to walk around the coals three times, and try again. The cooling effect of wet feet surely evaporated quickly during the long walk across the coals that took eight to ten steps, depending on how fast the devotee moved.

I am a huge skeptic of "made for tourists shows," so I really looked for deceptive behavior, but couldn't find much. I did see that the devotee's feet were covered in water before walking over hot coals and dipped in milk afterwards. I think the milk helped sooth the very hot, and presumably blistered, feet although I didn't see blisters on any feet. But then, I didn't ask. I couldn't muster the courage to ask to inspect a devotee's foot. I felt this was an invasive request and I really didn't want to see blistered feet anyway.

I also noted facial expressions as devotees crossed the pit, the faster devotees ran the more contorted their facial expressions were. The final stroll across the coals was completed by the priest. Then the coals were extinguished with milk and water.

I was exhausted after watching the fire-walking ceremony; I wondered what it was like to be a devotee. Witnessing the power of someone else's belief (or the power of one's mind) in the form of a trance and the ability to block pain (how else could someone walk across burning coals?) was taken to a new level that day.

WILDLIFE

I have had an interest in birds, wildlife, and animals from a young age. In the USA, we are fortunate to have many national parks and wildlife sanctuaries. Something I took for granted, until I saw other parts of the world. It was a luxury (sad but true) to see the different types of shore birds in New Jersey, elk in Arizona, and tadpoles grow into frogs in a pond near my house in Connecticut.

In contrast, I didn't see much wildlife or birds in developing countries. They were either eaten for survival (I still have visions of roasted rat in Laos and guinea pig in Peru) or their deaths a consequence of pollution or encroachment of habitats (this could be said of developed nations as well). Everywhere humans populate, they push everything else out. At times, I was ashamed at the pure arrogance and neglect we inflict on animals and the environment.

At other times, I was filled with amazement and astonishment at the resilience to survive. I honestly don't know how Mother Earth keeps up with our insatiable appetite for natural resources that we just take without much thought for future generations.

There are a few places in the world where wildlife survives and thrives.

In those places, it was a delight to let the world take center stage.

Australia

In Singapore, I happened to wander into a bookstore to browse and found a gem of a Lonely Planet publication on the wildlife of Australia. On a whim, I also bought a small pair of binoculars, and that was how my wildlife safari through Australia began. That book steered our travels through Australia over the next year.

The southern hemisphere is a land of opposites – the sun is to the north, the moss grows on the south side of the trees, the snow melts on the north side of the slope, the seasons are reversed, and most of all (at least for me) the constellations in the sky are different. Some constellations like the Southern Cross can't be seen in the northern latitudes of the northern hemisphere because of the curvature of the earth. The Southern Cross can be seen in the tropical latitudes for a few hours a night in winter and spring in the northern hemisphere.

Camping has its perks. At night I would always orientate myself in relation to the Southern Cross. If you don't know what the Southern Cross constellation looks like, take a look at the Australian and New Zealand flag that is the Southern Cross.

The island of Tasmania is located to the south of the city of Melbourne in the state of Victoria. After completing a ride down the "Great Ocean Road,'" and seeing koalas for the first time in the wild, we took a ferry to the north side of the island, and rode in a counter clockwise direction for nearly six weeks.

St. Clair National Park, located in the western central section of the island, is known for its abundance of wildlife. I planned to see as much as I could while there for a couple of days. To my delight, as sunset approached pademelons (a member of the marsupial family but smaller than kangaroos and wallabies) wandered out from the bushes near our tent. Momma was out eating at dusk and to my amazement a baby (called a joey by the Aussies) burst out of her pouch to have a peek outside. Minutes later, a wombat scurried by. I knew then it was well worth the effort to get there.

The wombat, marsupials, is the world's largest burrowing mammal, and is found solely in Australia. It resembles a small bear; this one was light brown. My love affair with the Australian wildlife had begun.

In the morning, we took a short hike to Platypus Bay to see where the platypuses lived. We returned around dusk hoping to see these elusive creatures because that is the time when they are known to come out and play. I knew what to look for in the wild after seeing a stuffed platypus (a sad ending for the fella) in the visitor's center.

The platypus is a semi-aquatic mammal found in eastern Australia and Tasmania. It (along with the echidna) is a monotreme, the only mammal that lay eggs instead of giving birth. The platypus is a strange creature: its head, bill, and webbed feet are similar to a duck while the rest of its body looks like an otter with a beaver-like tail. It is so odd looking that early scientists thought they were a hoax (poor creature didn't get any respect). They are bottom feeders and scoop up larvae, worms, and shellfish with their bill, store their food in their cheeks, and return to the surface to smash and consume their meal.

We went back to Platypus Bay around 7 p.m. and didn't have to wait but ten minutes before I spotted a little guy in my binoculars. He surfaced, dove down, and came back up again; it seemed like he was doing the back stroke when he resurfaced. Then he was gone, not to be seen again for the evening.

I was ecstatic, thrilled, and on high alert. Seeing the strange platypus in its own habitat put me into exploration mode. It spurred me on to investigate my surroundings, including the nearby forest. By the time we left Platypus Bay, it was dark and prime viewing time for nocturnal animals.

On the way back, Tim and I saw plenty of pademelons (we call them kangaroo juniors), a bush tail possum native to Tasmania, and a very large muscular feral cat that we knew wasn't a native.

Asbestos Range National Park

Asbestos Range National Park (the name was recently changed back to the Aboriginal name of Narawntapu National Park) is located twenty-five miles (forty kilometers) east of Devonport, Tasmania. My map and book still called it Asbestos Range National Park. We camped near the visitor center to be closer to the animal habitat. Not far from our tent were a few wombat burrows.

Our new neighbors arrived close to sunset. I asked the kids, Pat and Jessy, ages four and six, if they wanted to see where a wombat lives. They responded with screams of delight. Mom and dad asked me to stay close to their camp and I agreed.

"Follow me then. Be quiet. We don't want to scare the wombats," I whispered. We walked over the bridge in silence. As I pointed down the dry creek I said, "See those holes over there. That's where wombats live. And look. Holy cow! (so much for being quiet) There's one now!" Just as we looked at the burrow, a large dark-brown wombat wandered out. We didn't mean to disturb the animals, but all three of us squealed.

I was now the pied piper. I enjoyed showing those children wombats, kangaroos, and birds as much as they enjoyed seeing them. Pat and Jessy followed me all over the park, waiting to see where the next animal would appear.

Later in the evening, their parents walked them down toward the bird blind. I was on a mission to see what would come out after dark. With the enthusiasm of a child I strolled into the wild with my flashlight. I bumped into our Australian family neighbors as they were walking out so I stopped to chat. As we stood there, I heard something running through the bush in my direction. The sound of whatever it was made me jump off the trail. Lucky I did, a huge running wombat narrowly missed colliding with me as he crossed the trail. Again, the kids squealed.

Joan, the mom, reported they had seen an eastern spotted quoll up the trail. As they headed back to camp I moved deeper into the forest. Eastern spotted quolls are carnivorous marsupials, the same as the Tasmania devil. They look like a weasel, are about the size of a medium cat, and have a brown coat with big white dots. I was in luck. As I came around a blind corner I saw three of them scamper down the narrow trail. By now it was getting very dark. I wanted to walk into the bush a little farther, but my instincts urged me to go back.

I turned, walked ten steps, and stopped in my tracks. A spotted eastern quoll was on the trail in front of me. When I pointed my flashlight on it, it didn't move. It was mesmerized by my light that had also attracted a swarm of bugs. To my surprise, the quoll took a few steps toward my light, stood on its hind legs, and grabbed an insect with its two front paws. It proceeded to eat the bug – crunch, crunch, crunch – and grabbed for another one. It wasn't afraid of me. It was so close to my foot, I expected it to sit on it. It grabbed dinner from my light beam for the next five minutes and then followed me down the trail toward camp until I came to the clearing. I was thrilled to have encountered the eastern spotted quoll; I felt my observation skills were improving. I fell asleep that night to the sounds of pademelons and wallabies hopping by our tent.

A baby wombat playing on a sand dune at Asbestos National Park, Tasmania, Australia.

Cindie Cohagan

Part 5 - Low Points & Lessons

Changing a flat tire near Cafayate, Argentina.

Chapter 13
Did You Get Sick on the Road?

This is an intestinal parasite and it's obvious how it hooks into its host.

Getting sick while traveling adds challenges such as being exposed to foreign germs and diseases, not knowing where or whom to get medicine from, and not being able to communicate with the doctor (I found this to be the most trying).

The most common aliment on the road was intestinal problems, from diarrhea to constipation. The latter rarely being a problem when we rode the bikes. My background in sanitation helped to prevent exposure to the worst waterborne diseases. Simple habits such as never brushing our teeth with tap water and filtering or boiling all our drinking water kept us healthy most of the time.

For me, these illnesses occurred infrequently, but I had other problems. A bladder infection in Peru sent me to the hospital in Puno. I got impetigo twice – in Ecuador and Peru. My most serious illness was shingles. I believe I would have gotten shingles had I stayed home, so in my mind that doesn't count as a travel illness. However, it played a major role in ending my travels.

Between the two of us, Tim was sick more often. Besides a few bike crashes that ended in road rash and skinned knees, he had stomach issues including bacteria and parasites that lasted for years. I honestly don't know how he coped with his problems and rode a bike too.

PARASITES

All through Australia, Tim's health appeared to get worse instead of better. In May 2007, when I first dragged him to a doctor, he tested positive for various bacterium and was treated with an antibiotic. However, he continued to have intestinal discomfort, and looked run-down to me.

In September 2007, Tim wasn't recovering from whatever sickness he had and I insisted we see a special travel doctor while in Auckland, New Zealand. Fatigue, a distended stomach, excessive gas, diarrhea, and constant hunger (beyond the usual amount for a cyclist even) were only a few of his symptoms. I had to get to the bottom of his problem. It was an effort to get Tim to the doctor again; I was such a pest he went along to appease me.

After a short wait, a doctor in her mid-thirties called us into her office. She quickly launched into a series of questions.

"What countries have you been to?" she asked.

I began to list them in chronological order, "Mexico, Guatemala, Honduras, Nicaragua, Costa Rica, Panama. That was four years ago."

"No. Recently," she interjected.

"Oh. OK. Thailand, Vietnam, China, Laos, Malaysia, Singapore, Australia, and New Zealand," I said.

"Did you drink the water?" she questioned.

"No, absolutely not. We carry a filter with us and we don't even brush our teeth with the local tap water," I said.

"Did you go swimming or drink a large amount of water while showering?" the doctor asked.

"When we were in Vietnam, we did a boat tour of a floating market on the Mekong River. When we pulled alongside another boat, I was drenched with river water and swallowed some by accident. Cindie was on the other side of the boat and didn't get wet." Tim answered.

"OK, I will add a test for a parasite called schistosomiasis. It's a flat or fluke worm. The test requires analysis of a urine sample for three days in a row and that sample has to be collected between noon and 3 p.m. every day."

"I will make sure he does the test right. Where do I drop off the samples?" I asked.

"Any one of the small clinics in town will take your sample," she replied.

"Thanks for your help," Tim said. I took him home and went to a nearby clinic to get the sample containers.

Four days later, the results came back positive. I cried with relief and grief at the same time: relieved we knew what was wrong and grief for not finding out sooner. Tim had suffered with a parasite for over two years and possibly longer. The thought of parasites growing larger and larger in his intestines made me nauseated. It must have been huge by now because we were in the Mekong River area of Vietnam in January 2005 and southern China (another possible source) in December 2005. It was now September 2007.

The timing of this new information couldn't have been worse. The results came back on Saturday afternoon and we were catching a bus to New Plymouth the next morning. This meant we had to get Tim's prescription filled in New Plymouth.

It took over a week to get his medicine. The trouble was the drug praziquantal (commonly used to treat worms in dogs and cats) is a controlled drug and hard to get in New Zealand (something to do with it being a catalyst for a party drug). The side affects (nausea, vomiting) were pretty bad; the more worms the worse the symptoms. At the pharmacy, Tim had to show his passport and sign for his prescription.

He took the new drugs, felt better for a few days, and then was sick again. To our frustration, he still wasn't cured. Weak, worn out, and downright tired of all the medicine I was feeding him, we went to a doctor at a clinic in New Plymouth. The doctor, an Indian, walked in and asked, "Why are you sick?"

"I still have a parasite I got in Vietnam and the prescription for the praziquantal I got from seeing a doctor in Auckland wasn't strong enough, and the parasite is back." Tim said, to the doctor.

"Don't worry. You can live with a parasite. Sixty percent of the people in India have parasites, and they live with them every day," he claimed while he wandered over to a large bookcase, pulled a book off the shelf, thumbed through it to a particular page and said, "See here. In this book there are many kinds of parasites."

We looked at a full-page ad for parasites. It showed a slew of nasty looking creatures. Some had gaping mouths with fangs. Others were really long and slender while some appeared to have horns. Science fiction writers could find a lot of inspiration from that page. It didn't inspire me; it only made me feel conquered and I could only imagine how Tim felt.

A feeling of defeat settled over me. This doctor knew about parasites and appeared to think it was OK to have them. He prescribed an antibiotic.

Tim followed the doctor's prescription and took the drug for three days. It was useless. It didn't remove the parasites and Tim was still suffering. True to my suspicions this doctor was no help. Frustrated, I brewed about what to do next.

In the meantime, the weather had cleared. We finally had a view of Mount Egmont, also known as Mt. Taranaki, (a dormant stratovolcano) for the first time in months. It was time to climb on our bikes and ride. Rather than go straight to the South Island, we rode back toward the middle of the North Island to a place called Rotorua.

But first, we stopped to go on one of New Zealand's best day hikes at Tongariro Crossing. It's famous for crossing between two volcanoes and having great views of Lake Taupo. Our hike got rained out, which turned out to be a blessing because we met a German doctor at our guesthouse that day.

We discussed at great length how parasites plague the system and to my relief she believed parasites are bad and should be eliminated. Her opinion matched mine. All three doctors – one in Australia and two in New Zealand – had not given Tim a large enough dose of praziquantal or mebendazole to kill all the parasites, so, with time, they returned. She explained that the parasites most likely had laid eggs and the first dose of antibiotics eliminated the adult population, but not all the eggs. Six weeks later a new crop of parasites were hungry and taking as much nutrition from the host as they could. Tim was malnourished and he looked it. Her advice was to wait two weeks and then start a dose of two hundred milligrams per day of mebendazole for fourteen days.

Two weeks later, Tim took his first dose of a new antibiotic. On the fourth day he passed pieces of some type of worm (it must have been gross). He continued to pass them for four more days. On the eighth day, he passed bigger pieces (really gross) about the diameter of my pinky finger and an inch and a half long (nearly four centimeters). Oh heavens, that had had a long time to grow. I guess the first three treatments didn't kill this parasite. Four days after finishing the medicine, I saw a transformation in Tim; he had more energy and his riding jersey had loosened.

SHINGLES

After being abroad for over six years, in May 2008 we arrived in Alaska, where it felt more like the new frontier than part of the USA. It was great to stay with family, but it was a busy time. It took many weeks to finish our book about cycling in South America. I was working long hours, packing for cycling from Alaska to the lower forty-eight, and after so much time off the bike, I was out of shape. All this stress took a toll on my body and while traveling in the Canadian Outback, I started feeling sick with a slight fever and fatigue. I also felt a bump on my lower back at about waist level that I thought was a spider bite. That "spider bite" turned out to be blisters related to shingles.

Once I realized what I had, I got an antiviral right away. During an examination at a small clinic in Teslin, Canada that confirmed I had shingles, I asked, "Can I still ride my bike?"

"If you can. Sure. Go ahead," he replied.

"What do you mean, if I can?" I asked.

"Well, if you can handle the pain."

"What pain?" I was at the beginning stages and didn't feel much pain. Still, the doctor prescribed a week of painkillers (I could have used two year's worth).

Well, that was easy. I was going to ride. What I wasn't prepared for was the pain associated with shingles. I had caught the infection early, but I didn't get away from the pain. The nerve endings in my left upper back were already damaged. I had a chronic ache in there. This pain wasn't alleviated by taking aspirin or ibuprofens either. The entire time I rode in the USA I was plagued with constant pain. It wasn't until two years later, when I had a checkup in India, that the doctor prescribed a combination of B vitamins and amino acids that the pain finally subsided.

Later, while in McLeod Ganj, I attended a short course on Buddhist meditation at Tushita Meditation Centre. Besides having a calming effect, I immediately noticed the pain had disappeared completely. I began to meditate daily, sometimes for only fifteen minutes. I have experienced only minor pain since, and when I do, I meditate longer, and my pain subsides. What a blessing to find a solution to a chronic problem.

Inside the temple at Tushita Meditation Centre, Dharamkot, India.

Chapter 14
Why Did You Stop Traveling?

The former British hill station, McLeod Ganj, India.

AUSTRALIA

I began my online journal years ago so my family could contact me in case of an emergency. That emergency happened while we were in Kakadu National Park, Northern Territory, Australia. My twin sister, Cherie, worked out our last known location and called the ranger station.

A park ranger spotted us on the road the next day and pulled us over. He jokingly said we were speeding and then said, "There is a family emergency, but I don't know which family." I immediately called Cherie from the park office and my brother-in-law, Scott, gave me the tragic news. My older sister, Debbie, had died in a car accident the day before (August 17, 2007). My heart was broken in an instant. My grief was almost too much to bear, so much so I had trouble breathing.

The kind ranger drove us thirty miles (forty-eight kilometers) back into town. To distract us from our grief, he told us incredible tales about Kakadu.

There were so many decisions to make in a such a short time that I ended up going home alone and met Tim later in Australia before we flew to New Zealand. The journey home took nearly two days, with over thirty-six hours in the air. I stayed with my mom in Pennsylvania for a couple of weeks.

INDIA

I knew my travels were coming to end when I began to think, "There must be more to life than this: riding a bicycle in third world countries, staying in cheap hotel rooms, eating in cheap restaurants, and never getting to know anyone. Eight and a half years of traveling and publishing three books while on the road, was enough for me. I needed a connection to someone, to something; I felt disconnected from my family, society, and people in general. I only knew one person and we had exhausted any meaningful or interesting conversations some time ago. I wanted to do something different, I felt I had a lot to offer, and I should do something because I could. I wanted to at least stop and give back a little; I had been given so much during my travels that I felt out of balance.

My questions soon became; *How do I adjust the way I live my life with the added knowledge of what I have learned on the road? And, can I live with less and be content like the many people I met on the road?* I knew a simpler life with fewer possessions reduced my stress. Material wealth is nice, but more and more material possessions didn't equate to my happiness. I needed to balance the give-and-take in my life. I wanted to stop doing all the taking and while traveling by bicycle, I felt like I was doing all the taking. With these thoughts in my mind, we landed in India.

On June 2, 2010, Tim and I arrived in McLeod Ganj; I was already tired from the Indian heat, and my five-day bout with "Delhi Belly" I got the day after I arrived in India. McLeod Ganj is a former British hill station. Unfortunately, it experienced a strong earthquake of a magnitude of 7.8 on April 4, 1905 and ninety percent of its population perished. The town was abandoned and wasn't inhabited again until the Dalai Lama sought refuge in India from the invading Chinese army in 1959.

Slowly, the town grew into what it is today: a mix of Tibetans, local hill tribe Indians, and Kashmiris. It's quite a unique town when you add the Buddhist expats and visiting backpackers who come for Dalai Lama teachings, yoga or massage courses. The town is populated with numerous Western, Indian, and Tibetan restaurants plus a handful of coffee shops with WiFi, Buddhist bookstores, trekking shops, and Internet cafés.

Since we were staying for nearly four months, we found an apartment at the base of a very long (I counted 252 steps) set of stairs. It was a workout getting back and forth to town daily, but I didn't mind. My yoga class was nearby, and so was my English conversation class.

Even though I hadn't initially wanted to come to India, I was happy to be there to take care of my medical concerns, rest awhile, work on the electronic versions of our three books, and attend a Dalai Lama teaching.

I was also curious about Buddhism. I had witnessed the practice of Tibetan Buddhism while riding in China, and looked forward to attending my first teaching, which was in August. It was a two-day teaching sponsored by the Vietnamese on the "Diamond Sutra." I didn't have a clue what he talked about, and the westerner I went with wasn't up for a question and answer session. One more teaching was scheduled before we planned to leave so I penciled in September 18, on my calendar.

In the meantime, I participated in my first English conversation class. My first student, Tashi, was a twenty-seven-year-old Tibetan Buddhist monk who had arrived from Tibet in 2003. His departure from Tibet was not your typical backpacker hop-on-a-bus journey.

Tibetans are fleeing oppression from the Chinese government. Consequently, Tibetans must cross the Himalayas on foot, which usually takes at least a month.

Tashi was the only member of his family who came to India; he made the passage with twenty other Tibetans. He really missed his family, but it was dangerous for him to return to Tibet, especially being a monk. The other students in class had similar stories, just as heart-breaking. I could empathize with them being separated from their families; I too missed mine, only my exile was self-imposed.

I enjoyed the company of my Tibetan students; I found them to be resilient and always joking around. Having met a few groups of refugees in my travels, I thought the Tibetans were doing quite well in McLeod Ganj. A handful of NGOs in town provided free English, French, German, and computer classes, run by volunteers.

I had settled into a nice routine of yoga three days a week, English conversation three days a week, some hiking to try and get back in shape, and fitting in work that included creating mobi files for the Amazon Kindle and epub files for Apple iBookstore.

In early August, two Tibetan friends invited Tim and me to get a blessing from a young lama (teacher) called 17th Gyalwang Karmapa, Oygen Trinley Dorje. He is the head of the Karma Kagyu School of Tibetan Buddhism, and most likely the next spiritual leader of the Tibetan people when the Dalai Lama passes. The next spiritual leader must be the head of one of the four schools of Tibetan Buddhism. Of the four spiritual leaders, the Karmapa is the youngest and therefore would most likely be able to lead until the next (15th Dalai Lama) is trained.

I invited two American friends to join us. I bought my first mala (similar to a rosary) and my Tibetan friends brought katas (white scarves) so we could all be blessed. We had a lovely meeting with a young spiritual leader with a big presence.

It was August 17; the three-year anniversary of my sister's death. I still missed her and had a deep ache in my chest whenever I thought about her. It was hard to believe I was still grieving. I didn't know what to do about the pain in my chest, all I knew was I didn't want it anymore, and thought maybe a little spiritual guidance would help. I asked a Tibetan friend to show me around Tsuglagkhang temple (also known as Dalai Lama temple). He agreed, and we went that afternoon.

First we lit a candle. That simple gesture felt familiar; I had lit many candles for relatives in my youth, only then it was in a Catholic church. Performing that ritual both relaxed me and made a connection between the two religions. We took a tour of the temples, visited Shakyamuni Buddha first and then the Kalachakra temple. Each temple was filled with large statues and thangka paintings (paintings on fabric, all of a religious nature). I loved the prayer wheels around the backside of the temple and the little room upstairs where we made an offering. I was surprised how familiar the room felt and I assumed I was relating it to my previous Catholic experiences. The tour of the temple eased my pain and heightened my curiosity in Tibetan Buddhism. I was familiar with prayer wheels from traveling in the Kham region of Tibet, however, I wasn't familiar with the deities represented by the statues and thangka paintings.

The next Dalai Lama teaching was on the "Heart Sutra," sponsored by the Singaporeans and coming up the week before we planned to leave. I had met more westerners in town and four of us planned to go together.

At this teaching I managed to understand a little more of what the

Monks saying prayers in the Kalachakra temple.

Dalai Lama was saying. During one part he talked about the importance of helping others and not just oneself. I could relate to this because I had been on the receiving end of generosity for years. While on the bike tour people were always helping me find something, feeding me and/or giving me a place to stay. I, however, didn't feel like I was helping anyone. I exposed them to a different culture for a short time, but that wasn't fulfilling enough for me. I took more than I had given. I didn't look forward to passing through Indian villages and towns collecting handouts and giving nothing in return. I wanted to give back to my fullest capacity and I didn't know how to do that without stopping my travels. That was not an option Tim wanted to explore right then.

At the end of each day's teaching, the Dalai Lama walked down a corridor with people seated on both sides of the aisle. Followers from all over the world lined up to receive a blessing from him. I was sitting at the very end of the aisle on his left. As the Dalai Lama came out of the temple he was immediately surrounded by monks, sponsors, and security. I could barely see him through the crowd. He slowly walked down the aisle, stopping, holding hands, and chatting with a few people on each side of the aisle. He strolled over to the left and began blessing everyone sitting in the front row, one by one. He held each person's hand for just a moment and then moved on to the next. Gradually, he moved down the line.

When he came to me he gently held my hand, and smiled at me. I was thrilled to receive a blessing and surprised by the softness of his hands, and the energy that radiated from them. My only thought was, *I know what love and compassion feels like*. I felt it in his hands. He moved on to one more person, and then made his way down the stairs and back to his residence. I was so moved by his blessing; it felt like the connection I was looking for. Not just to the Dalai Lama, but to humanity in general. It was time to stop and help others wherever I could.

The next day I took refuge and became a Buddhist. When I told Tim the news, he wasn't happy. He did say he thought Buddhism is a decent religion, but it is just that, a religion. He was more concerned with getting out the door and back on the road. I was happy to have found a spiritual connection, wanted to study more, and dreaded leaving the following week.

It was with great sadness when I said good-bye to my recently made friends and pointed my bicycle downhill toward new destinations. I didn't have long to be sad. I was busy navigating new towns, finding hotels, and completing the unfinished book conversions. On the bike, my body hurt again from the lack of exercise for the better part of eight months. My mind remained in McLeod Ganj, thinking of all the events that I had experienced there.

Tim and I were caught in a dilemma. I wanted to stop traveling; he never wanted to stop. I often cringed when I heard him tell people, "We are never going to stop traveling. We will just keep riding our bikes until our bodies give out." Well, my body gave out before his. Shingles had worn me down. I expressed my weariness to Tim and that I wanted to stop, but he didn't want to hear it. His response was, "It's time to go." Resentfully, I climbed on my bike and followed him down the road.

The rest of India was so different from McLeod Ganj. I felt like I had entered a new country, the real India, where cities were busy, noisy, and the men stared more.

After a week on the bike, we arrived in a town called Rewalsar or Tso Pema, a small Buddhist community with three monasteries, and many Tibetan restaurants. We stayed in a monastery guesthouse and, while having coffee in the café, I realized I didn't want to leave Buddhism yet. I had found something that really interested me and wanted to learn more. It was a Thursday afternoon and another Dalai Lama teaching was coming up in McLeod Ganj on Monday. I wanted to go to that teaching.

Tim wasn't happy when I broke the news that I didn't want to continue riding to Nepal, but instead return to McLeod Ganj. We agreed to meet again in three months. In hindsight, this decision was made weeks earlier, when I applied for and got a residence permit that allowed me to stay in McLeod Ganj on a tourist visa without leaving. This option was open to Tim as well, but when I applied for the permit and asked him to go with me, he refused. He said something about getting car sick on the way down to Dharamsala. The new permit meant I could stay in India long-term, and, due to the conditions of his tourist visa, Tim had to leave after six months. The decision had been made.

We separated our belongings. I gave him everything he needed to cross over into Nepal and he gave me a broken bungee cord to fix and bring back to him. I hopped in a taxi – a bus would have been too much with all my gear – and headed back to McLeod Ganj.

Through a series of discussions and events, some of which were beyond my control, my short-term separation from Tim turned into long-term. While Tim continued to bicycle tour in Nepal, I returned to the USA for a short visit, filed divorce papers, and made plans to return to McLeod Ganj for a long stay.

Changing from a nomad to an expat wasn't as easy as I had thought it would be. At first, I felt like I was in McLeod Ganj temporarily, my friends were temporary, and so was my apartment. I kept having these urges to leave. I still bought instant coffee, instant milk, peanut butter, and went out to eat often. Over the many miles and years on the road, I had forgotten how to cook.

My apartment was huge and a chore to clean. I had trouble sleeping at night because the barking stray dogs woke me until I reminded myself that I wasn't sleeping in a tent and could relax. Some of my habits, like listening for movement in the night, weren't necessary anymore. However, that habit kept me awake. My attention span was short and my need for exercise was great; I took to walking everywhere.

I got to know the locals better and found an odd community: western Buddhists, visiting Ph.D candidates, American retirees, NGO workers, Tibetan refugees, including government workers, monks, nuns, nomads, and Kashmiri businessmen. What I hadn't realized was all the years on the road had made me an open and trusting person. I immediately trusted people and that turned out to be a mistake. I had forgotten how easily cliques form in small towns and I didn't fit into any of them.

That didn't matter. I needed a rest from traveling while juggling a business. I was a little ill, I still experienced chronic pain in my upper back.

I also needed to digest everything that had happened to me over the past eight and a half years, including a divorce, and moving to a foreign country with no immediate plans for returning to the USA.

On the way to the main square, McLeod Ganj, India.

Chapter 15
Lessons from the Road

Pushing through the sand in Bolivia.

During my travels, there were some definite turning points – lessons that only the road can teach. This wasn't my first trip abroad and I thought I knew what to expect. The difference between riding a bicycle through a country and riding a bus is in the subtleties.

On the bicycle, you see, smell, and taste the countryside. Cyclists are approachable and where ever we stopped we interacted with people, sometimes large groups of them. Changes in languages, customs, and mannerisms were experienced instantly. Changes in weather, terrain, and wind direction were felt immediately. The intensity was so much more at a slow pace. Rather than experiencing a country by hopping from island to island, we got the flow of the land.

Riding a bicycle forced me to push myself to my physical limits, transforming my thinking from "I can't" to "I can." I had to accept that I wouldn't always know where I would sleep at night, but it would always work out. Slowing days down to a snail's pace also gave me an opportunity to enjoy the simple moments of joy and happiness, and learn that forgiveness is better than holding a grudge.

I know if I had stayed home, I wouldn't have had these experiences and opportunities to change my outlook on life. My biggest change was how I viewed myself and that happened early in the journey.

THE MYTH

I had seen poverty, but was never immersed in it. That immersion shattered a personal myth I had believed for a long time: I grew up poor, and more importantly, without the privileges that wealth brings with an emphasis on the privileged part. *Poor, poor, little ole me.*

Guatemala

We had been on the road for more than seven months when we entered Guatemala. We had seen poverty in Mexico, but the daily existence in Guatemala was even more basic.

Seeing how they live simply with hand-made rather than store-bought bricks, hand-sewn clothes, homegrown food, and using firewood instead of gas for heating, opened my eyes to what poverty means. Up until this time I was under the illusion that I had grown up poor.

I pondered for hours on the bike where this myth had come from. I had an interesting upbringing, and experienced both what I thought were poverty and wealth at a young age. I was fortunate to go to college because of my grades.

In college I met and mingled with the wealthy, people who lived in houses and drove cars beyond my wildest dreams. It was evident who came from a wealthy family, and who didn't, by how their education was paid for. Mine with grants and scholarships. Nonetheless, after too many beers and not enough studying, (in hindsight, I should have worked harder) I received a bachelor of science degree in geology.

Still I was poor, p*oor little ole me.* I didn't wear the latest fashions, or drive a fancy new car (I rode a bike, how telling of my future) in my youth. Even after getting an education and a good job, I still carried around a sense that I had missed out on something. This was my thinking until I rode my bicycle through the canyons of Guatemala and witnessed what true poverty and struggle are.

Poverty is a battle for daily existence with no hope of doing better for an entire lifetime. I was never that poor. I didn't grow up with an abundance of material goods, but I always had hopes and dreams. I also had an education that was more valuable than any material possession.

Seeing "real" poverty put my life into perspective. I questioned the self-pity I carried around with me because I grew up poor. I wasn't poor by a long shot. I was wrong all my life to think this was true. If I was incorrect about that what else was I mistaken about?

When I realized this, while in Huehuetenango, Guatemala, I was irritated with myself for being so stupid to believe such an illusion. I was clinging to the belief that I hadn't had enough.

What I had not had were a lot of material possessions as a child, but I had had everything I needed. Yet I felt deprived and entitled to more.

I didn't know what hardship was either. Life just seemed to be bad, because I was comparing the amount of toys and clothes I had with people who had more. As if toys and clothes are the only sources of happiness. They aren't. Acquiring them gave me instant gratification, and when that was over I was left feeling empty. It was time to get off the pity pot.

The moment I realized I had everything I ever needed was an epiphany, it changed my perception. I no longer believed I grew up poor; on the contrary, I know I had, and still have, a privileged life. This change in perspective lightened my heart and infused me with enthusiasm. I now see I have a blessed life. I feel fortunate.

I went to college, got an education, and rode a bicycle around the world – opportunities few women in this world have experienced. If I had never left the comforts of my western lifestyle, I would never have realized this, and would still be on the pity pot. This alone made the trip worthwhile.

Knowing I have everything I need meant I could let go of my survival approach to life. The lasting effect of taking my worries away and directing my thoughts toward others instead of myself was profound. That, added to the removal of distractions of a western lifestyle, such as working long hours and concentrating on acquiring material belongings, opened me up to have compassion for others, and at times, compassion for myself.

This was the beginning of my spiritual awareness (so blessed to have all the causes and conditions come together). Compassion for myself came when I had negative thoughts, like I'm not good enough. I transformed those thoughts to "I am so lucky to be able to have this experience."

Compassion for others came with an empathy that was so strong I ached, not for me, but for them, and my thoughts moved toward, *How can I help all these people who are suffering more than I am?*

BOLIVIA

I can is better than I can't

On the high altiplano of Bolivia the scenery is snow-covered glaciated peaks, the air is crisp and cool, and the terrain is wide open spaces. Road conditions there were challenging. I couldn't always look around and enjoy the scenery because I was navigating around pot holes, corrugated ruts, and deep sand. Add a headwind and I felt like we were going backward more than forward.

At 11,975 feet (3,650 meters) the altiplano's environment is harsh. Growing vegetables or grass to support cattle or a large human population is difficult. Finding a hotel every hundred miles (161 kilometers) was an unrealistic expectation.

November 27, 2003 was the second day in a row of pushing my bike through a long section of deep sand. The thought of giving up flashed through my mind. I looked behind me to see how much effort it would be to turn around. Too much, I decided. I looked forward and I couldn't see the end of the sand pit. I had no choice but to push.

Instead of mentally fighting the problem with *I can't do this or I want to go home* (to my surprise this one rarely came up) I started repeating a mantra, *I can, I can.* Repeating that mantra made all the difference. My body followed where my mind led it and I pushed my bike through the sand pit. When I rolled my front tire onto hard ground again, I felt like I could take on anything.

A positive outlook goes a long way in improving the outcome of a situation. Now, when I come up against a physically demanding circumstance, I think of the "I can" sand pit and I push on.

ECUADOR

Pushing through difficult times

In June 2003 we arrived in Ecuador after a three-month break from bicycling. It was both a breath of fresh air and a reminder that getting back into shape is painful. The terrain was either up or down and at an altitude near 11,975 feet (3,650 meters) as well. On one lonely climb, I was ready to call it a day. We steadily rose up the side of the mountain and at each turn in the road it became obvious that there weren't any flat places to camp.

"I'm getting tired. Can we start looking for a place to stay?" I asked Tim. The sun was setting and we were still riding.

"We will find a place soon, you'll see," he answered.

I didn't believe him. I assessed the lousy odds of our getting a hotel room soon, which meant we would be camping. All I could see were rocks, shrubs, and a dusty blue sky. All I could feel was a whipping wind that carried grains of sand that stung my face.

Exhausted, and not concentrating on what I was doing, I was almost blown off my bicycle when I rounded a corner straight into the wind. Still we climbed. My legs screamed in pain. My heart pounded from the altitude. My stomach, which ruled the roost, was empty, and sounded the alarm to stop. *But where? Where are we going to sleep?* On one side of the road was a two-hundred-foot (sixty-one meters) rock face, the other side dropped into oblivion. We pedaled on and then, miraculously, our camping spot for the night presented itself.

We found a small semi-flat spot, well more like gently sloping away from the road. Our feet pointed downward all night. It was windy, too; we had to hang on to everything or it blew over the side of the cliff. We found this out the hard way when a small blue stuff-sack blew past us into a dark abyss. In the end, I managed to get a decent night's sleep; I think it was out of pure exhaustion that I slept so hard.

That was one of the more difficult camping spots we ever found, usually it was easier. Throughout the many miles, hills, beaches, plateaus, mountains, lakes, cities, and villages we always found a safe place to sleep. Always. The road was a good teacher and the lesson was to stop worrying and let life happen. Such a simple lesson has since saved me so much anxiety and wasted energy. Slowly, I began to let go, relax, and let the magic of the road show itself.

VIETNAM

The benefits of forgiveness

We entered southern Vietnam not far from Phnom Penh, Cambodia and followed the Mekong River toward Ho Chi Minh City, formerly known as Saigon. Everything I knew about Vietnam was about the war that ended when I was a teenager. Now, in my early forties, I worried that the Vietnamese hated Americans. Contrary to my concerns, I never once felt hatred from a Vietnamese in all of Vietnam, including Hanoi. The most hatred I felt came from a European backpacker who was drunk; his over-emotional reaction didn't count. Still I wanted to know how the Vietnamese people felt about the war. I decided to ask.

While having dinner at a brand new restaurant, we met the owner who was going to university studying biotechnology and English. He taught us a few Vietnamese words like coffee is ca phe, thank you is cam ban, and how much? is baon hiêu? Then I boldly asked him, what do the Vietnamese people think about the Vietnam War?

Startled, he paused, and then said, "For the Vietnamese people that war happened in the past. They choose to look to the future, not the past."

"Hmm, l see. Well, are they still angry at Americans?" I continued.

He smiled and said, "No, we're not angry with Americans. You have nothing to worry about."

Relieved, I said, "Thanks for answering my questions."

At the end of our meal he brought out a plate of fresh fruit with grapefruit, custard apple (sweet), papaya, pineapple, and watermelon. It was his gift to us.

We traveled in Vietnam for close to three months and only met one angry local and he was drunk (alcohol seems to bring out the worst in people). Other than that people were always well-mannered. If they were angry I didn't see it. I occasionally met an overzealous tout, or a vendor changing the price, but never anger. The Vietnamese people had moved on.

Americans, on the other hand, had not entirely. I met more Americans in Vietnam than any other country I visited. Many were returning GIs (Government Issue and slang for USA soldiers) who were assisting the Vietnamese wherever they could. From starting NGOs to bringing in hospital equipment where it was needed. Somehow, the once opposing sides had put their differences aside and moved forward. Forgiveness at that level was beautiful to see. It showed me there is a better way to deal with tragedy than holding onto a past that can't be changed.

LAOS
The best gift of all - happiness

In the highlands of Laos, I had gotten so used to the Hmong children running out to the road to sing/yell, "sabadee" with all their heart that it didn't surprise me when I saw a group of children clustered together up the road. They looked the same from afar, but when I got closer I noticed a difference.

The first child in a line of three was on crutches. She leaned on her crutches while her legs hung loose from her hip sockets, dangling in the air, (she most likely had polio) but that didn't stop her from waving and yelling, "sabadee." The younger child next to her had a cleft lip but a grin from ear to ear. The child next to him appeared to be about ten years old and had downs syndrome. That didn't matter; he was jumping up and down and waving at me like his favorite dog had just come home. I realized that, in general, I hadn't seen many handicapped people in most of Asia. I wondered where the adults were who usually accompanied the other children I had met in Laos.

Then it occurred to me I was probably passing an orphanage, and a wave of concern rushed over me. These kids, who were in the most need, appeared to be abandoned and I worried about their situation. But that wasn't what the kids were expressing. They were waving and beaming; I could feel their joy at greeting a total stranger. My empathy, mixed with joy, was overwhelming. The sight of their suffering engulfed me with worry and distress. These children were obviously suffering from one disease or another yet they were there greeting me with enthusiasm.

I glided past those kids and felt like I had been given a big hug. I was helpless to do anything but wave and yell, "sabadee" back and that was all they wanted. I was so touched by their genuine desire to greet me, my heart swelled with gratitude. The simplest encounters in life can provide the most joy, if we take the time to notice them.

When I think back on this long and wonderful journey I have been on, I don't remember the many miles I pedaled. What touches me the most is the honest genuine interaction between human beings, the loving kindness we give to and receive from each other. Somehow those children, who appeared to be suffering on the outside, also had joy on the inside.

Cindie Cohagan

That day opened my heart to humanity a little more.

A friendly wave from a child living in Laos.

Chapter 16
End of Journey Reflections

Living with only what I could carry.

I never expected to stay in India. I didn't want to go in the first place; I went to address my health issues. In that process, I became interested in Buddhism and disenchanted with the magic of bicycle touring. The shiny bits had worn off.

What was the impact of the journey on me? The trip pushed me both mentally and physically. I was given the opportunity to assess my lifestyle and make changes. Those changes stuck because the expedition was a long one and new habits could become ingrained. I don't think major life changes can occur in a month.

I settled in McLeod Ganj, India and began to digest what my trip and my life were all about.

What happened to that nervous woman who set out to see the world on a bicycle? The one who was afraid of dogs, tunnels, guns, and of getting robbed (OK, that was Tim's fear not mine). I grew, I faced my fears, and learned most of them were of my own making. I am more of a risk-taker now than I was when I started. Better to try and fail than not try at all.

I have always been a people person and that trait was amplified on the trip. As a matter of fact, the trip amplified all my traits. Just goes to show you can't run away from anything because it follows you anyway.

The expedition, as I like to think of it, forced me to grow in ways that I never would have if I had stayed in the USA and continued to work as a geologist. I never would have understood the privileges that come with being a westerner, or how lucky I am to have an education, or what poor really means, or how kind and generous most people are in the world.

I began with fear in my heart and ended with warmth in its place and a desire to help others. I also think the world is my home, not just the USA. The world has gotten smaller, and with the way the Internet and phone communication are these days, the barriers we call countries are dropping.

When I am old and look back on my life, I will not regret launching into the unknown to see what was out there. I will never think it was a waste of time. I am glad I did it when I did because some circumstances, like living in a tent in Australia for nearly a year, I would never do again.

I genuinely like people and because I do, I trust them, and give them the benefit of the doubt. Across the many miles and smiles, I learned to detect insincerity, regardless of nationality or culture. Consequently, I trust my gut feelings about people, one hundred percent of the time.

It wasn't all roses out on the road either. I saw my share of bad people; for some reason Tim seemed to attract them. Most of the time they had had too much alcohol and were searching for money to buy their next drink. I have seen the results of too much drinking and drugs; it destroys communities, and puts the burden of everyday life on the people (usually women) who were not high on coca leaves, or drunk on pulque (a fresh-made beer in Mexico). Over and over I saw desperate people act selfishly. Yes, the world has people who behave badly. If you look carefully, it's usually out of desperation, such as a drug addiction, extreme poverty, boredom, greed, or a sense of entitlement. However, the good far outweigh the bad.

My belief that people are basically good was tested over and over again in many countries by young, middle-aged, and old, rich or poor. Over time, my numerous encounters with strangers reinforced that belief, rather than dispel it.

I often think of people who helped me in times of need, like giving me water when my bottles were empty. Giving me a place to sleep indoors when every inch of land was filled with cattle or a home, and, in hindsight, it probably was dangerous to be camping. Giving me food when I was riding up a steep hill. Once while in the Himalayas, a car came annoyingly close to me; the window rolled down, and out stretched a hand with an orange. My irritation immediately changed to delight. I gratefully took the orange, and ate it later.

We met a Chinese family at an outdoor restaurant in the Kham region of Tibet that served only noodles. After two bowls of noodles, they could see we still needed to eat and wanted to help. They went to their car and gathered whatever they had – bread, apples, and cokes – and handed everything to us like an offering. We were so hungry we ate everything in an instant.

So many strangers gave me a smile (especially New Zealand) when I was sad.

Or gave me encouragement to pedal on when I felt worn out (this was Tim on more times than I can count).

When I think back over the whole journey, I feel connected with many human beings at a basic level. I have come to view my experiences as a blessing, my heart is filled with gratitude and joy and the warmth in my heart dispels fear and suspicion.

LESS IS BETTER

Being content with what I had reduced my stress, worry, and anxiety. Witnessing that people like the farmers in Mexico and the sheep herders in Bolivia can be happy with very little was eye opening. They didn't appear to want more than enough food, clothing, and shelter. While living on the bike for so many years, I learned to be content with less and now extra material possessions feel like a burden.

This was completely the opposite of how I felt and behaved when I was working mega hours as a geologist. My attitude was along the lines of: I deserve this because I work so much. I had a sense of entitlement to buy stuff, to indulge my wants and desires because poor me was working so hard. I didn't see the vicious cycle of working to buy possessions; I had become a slave to my monthly payments.

What I thought I was entitled to (owning a car, a house, or having a hot shower) were privileges most people in this world don't have. I was open to learning this after I got off the poor me pity pot. If that hadn't happened, I don't think I would have been able to see the joy of having less. I became aware of this when I stopped thinking of myself, but of those around me. If I hadn't seen how exaggerated and self-centered my idea of growing up poor was, I probably never would have changed.

I finally realized that having belongings takes energy to acquire, use, and secure and when that takes more of my time and energy than I want to give, I know these items are not worth it. I free my mind by not having too many belongings.

The process of living with less is ongoing. Sometimes, I am still plagued with accumulating "stuff." How did I ever end up with three heaters in India? A fear of being cold maybe? I didn't need them all at once. So I gave one away, lent one out, and kept one. At least someone else could use it when before it was stored under my bed. What a waste to have possessions and not use them.

HEALTH

The bike expedition was a fountain of youth for me because I got healthy. I still have hypoglycemia, but I don't have diabetes. My cholesterol and triglycerides dropped, my blood pressure normalized, and my energy and endurance increased. Daily exercise cured my erratic blood sugar levels and my insomnia. Sleep came easy after hours on the bike.

I rather enjoyed getting in good shape so a flight of stairs didn't take my breath away. Given all the places I went, and all the food I ate, I had relatively few ailments and only a few minor crashes on the bike.

Tim, on the other hand, constantly battled stomach ailments from the very beginning; he was more sensitive to changes in diet than I was. He also had a couple major crashes, one in Peru and one in Australia. I don't think this shows poor bike handling skills on his part, I think he rode at the edge of his abilities more.

I have never been a super athlete, never will be, even after riding my bike around the world. Pushing myself to my physical limit taught me to listen to my body. I found I was more resilient than I imagined, many times my limitations were mental not physical.

My eating habits changed. I now watch what I eat rather than think I can eat anything. Through the sequences of on and off the bike, I learned to eat to maintain my weight. It wasn't easy paring down the quantity of calories I consumed when riding the bike and then stepping off to write a book. At first my weight yo-yoed and I felt unhealthy.

Now I maintain my weight the best I can by walking every day. Life is a balance between what we want to do and what we should or must (have to) do. I value my health over an income, therefore I put more time into exercise than I did before.

Some people ask if I will bike tour again. Yes, of course, I will. I love to ride my bike. I just won't do it for so long next time.

EDUCATION

Every morning I hear the sweeping sound of a broom, a woman cleans the balcony of the building next door. Every morning this is all she does, sweep; this is all she will ever do.

I am grateful to be a woman born in the West. The opportunity to get an education that leads to a better life doesn't come to everyone born on this planet. I did well in school because my mother insisted I do my homework; at the time, I didn't see the point, but she insisted that I do the best I could. Looking back, this was one of the greatest lessons my mother instilled in me, the importance of an education. I was the first woman (my twin a very close second) in my family to go to college.

Only a small number of women in the world have an education beyond high school; I am in an elite group. With an education I acquired financial liberation.

It is a privilege to have the freedom to choose the direction of my life. It didn't look that way to me when everyone around seemed to have the same option, but it is a privilege all the same.

Education is what changes the way people think and what they do more than anything else.

Education is a gift that never stops giving. Once you have it, no one can take it away from you, ever. It saddens me to see people who can go to school, but don't because it takes too much work. Honestly, you're worth it, take the time and energy to learn.

I DIDN'T CHANGE, MY PERCEPTION DID

The big change for me is how I perceive life; I look at it through a different pair of eyes. Rather than fussing about what I don't have, I count my blessings every day. With this good life, I should help others who are not as fortunate. With this education, I should help people who don't understand the problem. With this fearlessness, I should live my life to its fullest and take the risks. Without risks there are no rewards.

For me, it is far worse to sit in a house and worry about what might happen than it is to get out the door and experience a full life. Through all the ups and downs, and loss of family, friends, and a husband, I don't have any regrets. I have been given a huge gift from the road: a warm heart that dispels fear and suspicion. I have also gained the ability to see opportunities, and the confidence to say, "I can." I am grateful for what I have, and with that appreciation is joy. I still perceive people to be good, and look for the good in everything I see. As the Dalai Lama says, "Choose optimistic, it feels better."

All these are gifts that money can't buy; you can't go out and get this information off a shelf or google it on the Internet. Only experience can change the way we think, and the trip around the world was a boatload of experience I am still learning from. The challenge will be to keep these lessons and reflections in mind as I navigate through a less nomadic life. Now, to take all that I have learned and apply it to the next chapter in my journey.

Epilogue

My journey began with shedding most of my material belongings and simplifying my life to what I could carry on a bicycle. Without that step I would never have been free to explore the spiritual side of life, I would have remained mired in my belongings and never gotten beyond working to gain material possessions.

It was in Guatemala when I realized what being poor really was and I had never been poor. Throughout the rest of my travels I was overwhelmed with the human condition: poor living situations like people living in shelters that barely protected them from the rain and cold; no access to clean drinking water is common for the majority of people in this world; infant mortality is high in many places because they don't understand they are polluting their own drinking water; disease is rampant and life expectancy short in areas with little education. Women carry the extra burden of raising children and keeping families glued together. For the most part humans are in a suffering state. Witnessing the unending suffering of the human condition, I developed compassion for my fellow man.

From the very beginning I was drawn to ancient cultures and spiritual places as if I was looking for answers there. I have had the blessing to have visited numerous Mayan ruins, the most amazing Christian churches, walked parts of the Inca Trail, wandered through a stunning Hindu turned Mahayana Buddhist site called Bayon at Anchor Wat that retained a spiritual enlightened feeling even as the country was plunged into the evils of war and genocide. I visited an empty Tibetan Buddhist monastery where I could still feel the energy of praying monks from centuries gone by, marveled at the primitive yet highly spiritual Aboriginals in Australia who still put an emphasis on their spiritual journey called a walk about, the Maori of New Zealand who still lived in small villages, tattooed their faces, and used Tohungas people who were spiritual guides and protectors, visited First Nation totem poles that passed on stories of their ancestors, and watched Native American pow wow dances. All these spiritual places drew people together rather than apart.

I also saw the resilience of humans in all environments, from the high Himalayas and Andes down to the tropics of Costa Rica and Thailand, where people found a way to work together, and take care of each other. I pondered how and why people survived, and the answer was always through a spiritual connection be it Christian, Hindu, Muslim, or Buddhist or some other religion I didn't understand.

The years of travel had stripped me of my attachment to material possessions (for the most part), opened my eyes to our precious human existence ,developed my compassion for my fellow human, taught me we are all going to die someday, so I'd better figure out a way to deal with it, and I am accountable for my own actions and responsible for my own happiness.

When I arrived in McLeod Ganj I was tired, worn out, and lacked a sense of purpose and connection. What I found was a spiritual connection that filled that empty spot that I've always had.

I study Buddhism because it answers the questions I've always asked, gives daily guidance on how to be a better person, is compatible with my scientific way of looking at life, and connects me with my fellow man.

FOOTNOTES

1 - El Paso Business Frontier – Federal Reserve Bank of Dallas, El Paso Branch, Issue 1 - 2004
2 - William Lloyd George, Time – World, Hmong Refugees Live in Fear in Laos and Thailand, July 24, 2010.
3 - Agents Respond to Traffic, Patrol Closer to the Border, Perla Trevizo, Arizona Daily Star, August 19, 2013.

About the Author

Cindie Cohagan is an American writer/publisher currently living in India. She traveled the world by bicycle for over eight years before landing in Dharamsala. Her publishing company is Drifting Sands Press.

If you want to get an automatic email when Cindie's next book is released, sign up for her email newsletter at www.driftingsandspress.com. Your email will be kept private, never sold and you can unsubscribe at any time.

Word of mouth is essential for any author to succeed. If you enjoyed the book please consider leaving a review on Amazon. A short review is fine and greatly appreciated.

Get in touch with Cindie on Facebook or send her an email: driftingsandspress@gmail.com

OTHER BOOKS BY CINDIE COHAGAN
Finding Compassion in China: A Bicycle Journey into the Countryside

ABOUT THE PUBLISHER
Drifting Sands Press is an independent publisher specializing in spiritual journeys and out-of-the-ordinary life paths. Come see some of the other authors at Drifting Sands Press or visit our Drifting Sands Press Facebook page. Contact Drifting Sands Press via email: driftingsandspress@gmail.com

www.ingramcontent.com/pod-product-compliance
Lightning Source LLC
Chambersburg PA
CBHW070455100426
42743CB00010B/1624